Young People's
Book of the Constitution

Young People's Book of the Constitution

L. L. BLAKE
of the Middle Temple and
Gray's Inn, Barrister

THE SHERWOOD PRESS

First published 1982

Reprinted 1983

©L. L. Blake 1982

The Sherwood Press Ltd, 88 Tylney Road, London E7 0LY

ISBN 0 907671 04 7

Set in Baskerville by Bookens, Saffron Walden, Essex
Printed and bound by The Burlington Press,
Foxton, Cambridge

For
Charmian
and Emma and Andrew

Contents

Introduction (Mainly for Adults)

This book is intended for young people who are just beginning to ask questions about citizenship. It is such a pity if they do not know about the rich heritage and principles of their constitution before they actually do become citizens.

As Lord Denning has observed, it is a subject much neglected in our schools (outside of 'O' and 'A' Level syllabuses); whereas in the United States of America it is very thoroughly taught.

One purpose of this book is to set out some of the literary jewels which lie at the heart of our constitution: words which our founding fathers and statesmen have used to direct us through the ages. Some of these quotations may be difficult for the younger readers—but it is the *sound* of the words themselves which will send them off on a pursuit of the riches of language.

Looking at the map of the world today, the most alarming feature is the growth of tyrannical governments. Here, in the English-speaking nation, shines a beacon light of freedom. What finer challenge and purpose can our children have than to maintain that lamp for the benefit of humanity!

Gray's Inn
July 1982

1

What is the Constitution?

> It is a constitution made by what is ten thousand times better
> than choice; it is made by the peculiar circumstances, occasions,
> tempers, dispositions, and moral, civil, and social habitudes of
> the people, which disclose themselves only in a long space of
> time. It is a vestment which accommodates itself to the body.—
> *Edmund Burke*

What is meant by the word 'constitution'? It is good practice to
look up words in a dictionary, such as the *Shorter Oxford*, or,
better still, the great volumes of the *Oxford English Dictionary*,
which give examples of how words have been used over the
centuries and of how parts of words have come together to
form an idea that rules the lives of men. Also there is Skeat's
Etymological Dictionary, which shows where words have come
from.

So let us examine the word 'constitution'. Professor Skeat
tells us it is made up of two Latin words, *con-* or *cum*, meaning
'together'; and *statuere*, meaning 'to place or to set'. *Constituere*,
in Latin, means 'to stand together', 'to establish'. The word
conveys the idea of what keeps us together, what we share in
common, what enables us to think and act in the same way.

If we go back far enough we come to one of the oldest and
finest of human languages, Sanskrit, where the word is *stha*,
meaning simply 'to stand'. This word *stha* has given rise to a
tremendous number of words to do with Man and his purpose
on this planet, for Man alone among the animals stands and
looks ahead of himself fearlessly. Thus we have words like
'understand', 'state', status, 'statute', 'constitution', and so on.
They describe not only *how* a man stands but *where* he stands;
for this is important, too. A man, given office such as that of the
Pope, clad in fine robes and standing and speaking on a

balcony high over St Peter's Square in Rome, can command the allegiance of millions of human beings.

There must be a constitution for the whole of mankind, of men past, present and future, which they all share in, and which makes them men rather than animals.

In the Sanskrit language the word 'man' meant 'to think'. Man is thinker. This distinguishes him from animals: he is given the power to reason, to use his mind. Only Man has the ability, through mind and speech, to express the love and life and knowledge of his Creator, and to form and transform the world in which he finds himself. It is a very great power indeed. In the Book of Genesis, in the Bible, we find God giving Man dominion over the earth and all that lives on it. Men can either use that power for their own selfish ends, when they despoil the planet and the result is misery for themselves as well as all other creatures; or they can use it for the good of creation.

If we look at a map of the whole world we see the planet Earth, the home of Man, where he has dominion under God. All kinds and types of men live here: they have differently coloured skins; some brown, some black, yellow, white. They worship their Creator in different ways; they have different laws and customs; above all, they have different languages. The map itself shows us that men are grouped in many countries. Each country has its own limits, shown on the map as 'boundaries' or 'frontiers'. Sometimes the boundaries are the seas, as around the British Isles; sometimes they are rivers, or mountains, or even imaginary lines drawn through the desert, as in Africa.

These countries have different names. Each one has a capital city, from which roads and railways connect up the various parts of the country, just as the brain in the human being is connected up with parts of the body. Perhaps the atlas will give the flags of the countries: these flags are considered to be of special importance, and are saluted and honoured with military guards. They are symbols of the countries to which men belong, and which they recognise as being bigger and more important than themselves and their families.

But why are there so many countries? Why cannot all men live together as one big family?

The answer is, we do, actually. We depend on each other, for making and exchanging goods, for ideas, for music, art and literature. Everyone has something to contribute to this process. When men co-operate and work together, happiness arises. All men, everywhere, want happiness: and when it arises they all share in it. We remember the stories which enchanted us when we were very young, stories such as *The Sleeping Beauty* and *Cinderella*: they all end with 'and they lived happily ever after'.

The great English lawyer, Sir William Blackstone, who lived in the eighteenth century, said that the rule of obedience to God was very simple, that each man should pursue his own real happiness. But note the word 'real': we cannot be happy if we lie, cheat or steal from others, or abuse them.

The nature of Man is to be happy. We are told that bliss is the nature of the Creator. So the two natures are the same. Trouble begins only when men want happiness just for themselves. When a baby is born, he or she seems to lack for nothing and does not want to hold on to anything; but very soon the small child starts to demand '*my* toys'. Then separate natures come into play, for men start to want separate things. 'Nature' has to do with the desires a man is born with, for it comes from the Latin word *natus*, meaning 'born'.

From very early on men seek their own happiness in a variety of ways, and many different natures reflect these desires. They seek happiness for themselves and for others whom they know and live with, their families and the people with whom they share the same language, laws and religion. These are what cause 'nations' to arise from the wholeness of mankind. Nations are to do with different languages, laws and religions.

The word 'nation' shares a common root with the word 'nature' for both are derived from *natus*, being born. And we should expect people of different nations to have different natures. The boy or girl who comes from France will have a whole set of different attitudes from the boy or girl who was

born in England. They are not in any way essentially different—
they are members of the human race—but the things that they
consider important, the things they value, will vary. For
example, it is often said that an English man or woman is born
with a great love of, and desire for, freedom. This is a
characteristic of their nature, and of the English nation.

The different values and attitudes will be shown in people's
laws and languages: less so in their religions, even though the
way they worship may be different, because religions have a
more unifying effect among men and the nations to which they
belong. The great religions of the world are few in number.
The French boy or girl and the English boy or girl probably
share a Christian background.

We begin to see the marvellous order of humanity unfolding.
First, the essential unity of mankind itself; then the few, great
religions which give rise to civilisations in which men live; then
the nations which adopt these religions and have laws and
languages based on them; then the many different 'states'
which are the countries shown on the map; and so to the
families and the individual man or woman.

Sir William Blackstone, the lawyer already mentioned, had
this to say:

> . . . man was formed for society; and as is demonstrated by the
> writers on this subject, is neither capable of living alone, nor
> indeed has the courage to do it. However, as it is impossible for
> the whole race of mankind to be united in one great society,
> they must necessarily divide into many; and form separate
> states, commonwealths and nations; entirely independent of
> each other, and yet liable to a mutual intercourse.

Nations are larger than states. Nations have more to do with
people than states, which are confined within the boundaries
shown on the map. People of one nation can spread across the
whole world and live in different countries or states, as the
English have done. What brings them together is a common
language, law and religion. You will find Jewish people,
example, living in many states: they follow the laws of
countries in which they live and speak the various languages,

but they keep to the Judaic religion and have their own laws and language as well. This is true also of Indian and Arabic people who come to live in England.

This book is about the nature of the English-speaking people. But it is also about the constitution of a particular state—the state of England, and what holds it together. We refer nowadays to the islands on which we live as the 'United Kingdom of Great Britain and Northern Ireland', because they include Scotland and Wales, as well as England. But the form of government by which we stand together is essentially English. The first thing we have to recognise is that the state is much bigger than the individual and his family. It is a kind of person. Each state is a member of the family of mankind. Just as we are members of our families, so each state has a body (its people) and a mind (its government). In fact we often hear a particular country being called 'she'. For example, 'China is a vast country. *She* has many natural resources.'

In a way this is quite understandable. We are born into a particular nation and share its nature and its values. The state gives us a home and educates us and gives us work to do. So it is like a mother to us.

Twenty-five centuries ago, in Athens, the philosopher Socrates accepted that he would have to die, after being convicted on false charges prepared by his enemies. Crito, his friend, visited Socrates in his cell and urged him to escape, not understanding why Socrates should suffer death when he had done no wrong. But Socrates refused. He would not escape, he said, because that would set the bad example of disobeying those laws with which one did not agree. Then Socrates imagined the laws of Athens speaking to him:

> Consider, Socrates, if we are speaking truly that in your present attempt you are going to do us an injury. For, after having brought you into the world, and nurtured and educated you, and given you and every other citizen a share in every good which we had to give, we further proclaim to every Athenian, that if he does not like us when he has come of age and has seen the ways of the city, and made our acquaintance, he may go where he pleases and take his goods with him; and none of us

laws will forbid him or interfere with him. Any of you who does not like us and the city, and who wants to emigrate to a colony or to any other city, may go where he likes, and take his goods with him. But he who has experience of the manner in which we order justice and administer the state, and still remains, has entered into an implied contract that he will do as we command him.

So Socrates drank the poison which had been awarded him under the laws of the state.

We shall be referring to Socrates again in this book, through the teachings of his pupil, Plato. The ideas recorded by Plato have had a tremendous effect for good in the history of our own and other nations. But one thing you may already have noticed from the above extract: how Socrates, a master-teacher of the human race, speaks from the level of all mankind. He uses reason. He truly thinks. What he says about the laws of Athens could be said about the laws of any country, at any time. This is how we get a sense of the point of view of a master-teacher, because it takes into account the individual and the laws of the state in which he lives. It also goes much higher, seeing, as it does, that the whole of humanity will suffer if the laws which men adopt are not obeyed. It is better, says Socrates, that one individual suffers death, even unjustly, rather than set the laws at nought and encourage others to disobey. That can only end in confusion, bitterness and warfare.

Of course, this teaching has often been misunderstood. There have been, and still are, dictators and tyrants who say that the state is all-important and the individual is worth nothing. Under this idea they have killed and maimed millions of innocent people. But the results have spoken for themselves: misery, poverty, and the almost complete absence of beauty and light in such tyrannies.

In fact, it is better to look at it the other way: the state exists to serve the individual. Service is always from the strong to the weak. As we read this book, we shall see how men and women in government are there to serve the people. The Queen above all, for her service is absolute and all the time. Government is meant to conduct us towards happiness and knowledge, which we realise through using the talents and skills we have been given, for the benefit of others. If the state provides the conditions in which the talents of the individual can flourish, then he will grow stronger and will come under the duty to serve those weaker than himself.

So there are these various levels at work, within the wholeness of humanity. And each level reflects the others. The state is a reflection of the individual. It is the individual made large. When we read, as we shall do, of all the marvellous pageants and displays of Her Majesty's government, we shall find it is rather like watching coloured slides. Yet the beauty and the intelligence and the splendour of it all are really only reflections of the powers of the mind in each of us. People in the past, working for the good of mankind, have developed these ideas, these images, to remind us that these powers exist in everyone. The best kind of government is self-government, where a man realises that he has a Queen and a Parliament and Judges all in himself, and that each of us is a little state. Plato talks about this in the book called *The Republic*:

I told them what I really thought, that the search would be no easy one, and would require very good eyes. Seeing then, I said, we are no great wits, I think we had better adopt a method which I may describe in this way; suppose a short-sighted person had been requested by someone to read small letters a long way off; and someone else told him that he had seen the very same letters elsewhere written larger and on a larger scale—if they were the same and he could read the larger letters first, and then proceed to the lesser—that would have been thought a rare piece of good fortune.

Very true, said Adeimantus; but how does the illustration apply to us?

I will tell you, I replied; justice, which is the subject of our enquiry, is, as you know, sometimes spoken of as the virtue of the individual, and sometimes as the virtue of a State.

True, he replied.

And is not a State larger than an individual?

It is.

Then in the larger the quantity of justice will be larger and more easily discernible. I propose therefore that we enquire into the nature of justice and injustice as appearing in the State first, and secondly in the individual, proceeding from the greater to the lesser and comparing them.

That, he said, is an excellent proposal.

2

The English Constitution

Just before he died King Alfred spoke to his son Edward, and gave him good advice about taking care of the people when he became king.

I will tell you some of the words he said to Edward. Perhaps you will not fully understand them now, but pray remember them, because, when you are a man you will love to think of them, and to recollect that they were the very words of the best and wisest king we have ever had. The words are these—

'It is just that the English people should be as free as their own thoughts'.—*Maria, Lady Callcott*

The constitution of a nation is that which holds it together. Wise men give laws, language and a religion best suited to the people in their care. We shall see how it is done when we look at King Alfred.

First of all there are the people themselves. At the beginning of the Christian era, about two thousand years ago, the Romans came to the British Isles. The Romans were a highly civilised people, with developed laws, language and a religion of their own. They used their skills to build towns, forts and fine straight roads, the lines of which can still be traced today. The old British tribes resisted the Roman rule at first; but they came in time to enjoy the prosperity which strong, firm government brought them. As the Christian religion began to be adopted by the Romans, so it was introduced into this country.

Roman rule lasted in Britain for about three hundred years. It covered a large part of the British Isles: in the north, however, the Emperor Hadrian built a wall—which you can still see—for the purpose of keeping out the Pictish tribes from what is now Scotland. The Romans did not penetrate much beyond this wall, which they manned with their soldiers. It was a frontier of the vast empire which the Romans governed, extending throughout Europe, and which all started with the energy and intelligence of these people gathered together in the city of Rome in Italy. But then, the Romans themselves suffered invasions close to home; and they began to withdraw their soldiers from the outposts of their empire, from places like Britain. Gradually the Roman empire dwindled away. All nations have life-spans, just as individuals do. They are born, grow up, mature and die. It is just that the time-scales are different.

New invaders appeared in the British Isles. These were Angles and Saxons from what is now Germany. They treated the Britons ruthlessly, killing them and driving them westwards, largely into the country now called Wales. In fact, the Welsh language, which you can still hear spoken, is derived from the British tongue.

The Anglo-saxons are our direct ancestors. We get the name 'England' from the 'land of the Angles'. And the names of our counties, which are parts of the kingdom, reflect the coming of the Saxons: 'Sussex', the land of the South Saxons; 'Essex', the land of the East Saxons.

Tacitus, a Roman historian, wrote a book about these ancestors of ours, called *Germania*. He wrote it in about AD 100, so it is a very early account of the nature of the people who were to form the English nation. It is interesting because, in many ways, the character and attitudes of the English have not changed in all the years since he wrote his book.

Tacitus says that they have fierce-looking blue eyes, reddish hair and big bodies. But they do not particularly care for hard work and cannot bear thirst or heat. When they fight an enemy, the soldiers are gathered together from families which know each other very well, and therefore the men fight better because they can rely on each other.

Their kings do not have power to decide great matters by themselves but have to take the advice of everyone else. They have public meetings to decide them, at which all the men attend, but it takes them a long time to arrive, maybe even days before they can overcome their idleness. At these meetings the men take their seats fully armed. If a proposal displeases them, they shout their dissent; if they approve, they clash their spears. Waving their weapons about, says Tacitus, is the best means they have of agreeing with each other.

They like war and are not very good at peaceful activity, spending most of the time sleeping and eating. 'The boldest and most warlike men have no regular employment, the care of house, home, and fields being left to the women, old men, and weaklings of the family.

They live apart from each other in rough houses surrounded by open spaces. But they love feasting and entertaining. 'As soon as they wake, which is often well after sunrise, they wash, generally with warm water—as one might expect in a country where winter lasts so long. After washing they eat a meal, each man having a separate seat and table.'

Drinking and gambling are great sports with them. They get to know each other best when they have been drinking a lot; but they do not make any decisions until they have sobered up. Women are allowed to show their grief by weeping and wailing, but men should not do so.

Those are our ancestors, many centuries ago, as seen by the Roman, Tacitus. Some things have not changed, have they? The English still like to live in separate houses and sit apart from each other in buses and trains. What else is there about the English character as described by Tacitus, that you can still see today?

One especial quality which Tacitus observed in the people he wrote about was this love of liberty and strong independence. They were not very willing for someone else to tell them what to do. It took them quite a long time to come together for a meeting; and, once there, the king had to get their agreement if something important had to be decided.

As we shall see, this quality has meant much in the history of our nation. For one thing it has meant that English people do not take very kindly to officials interfering with their lives all the time; they like to run their own affairs. This is quite different from the Romans, whom we talked about at the beginning of this chapter. The Romans were highly organised and looked to the state to decide things for them. The state was more important than the individual.

This difference in nature was to give rise to the two great systems of law which we still have in the world today: the system based on Roman Law and the Common Law of England. You will find the Roman Law system in the countries of Europe, such as France, Germany and Italy. It arises from a Latin principle which, translated, says: 'What pleases the prince has the force of law.' In other words, if someone in authority tells you what to do, you do it. This, in itself, is not necessarily a bad thing. After all, there have to be people in charge of most of our activities, but the English have always considered it a better way of life to leave most of the decisions about how to act to the individual himself or herself. It means, of course, that the individual must act responsibly: that is, he or she must not hurt anyone else. The point is, to help other people, without being told what to do.

The great Common Law of England, which has spread across the world, to all countries in which English is spoken, grew out of the simple idea that every man or woman is utterly free to do what he or she wants, as long as it does not interfere with someone else's right to do the same. It is the law of duties: and the meaning of 'duty' is what is due to someone else. To give an example, you can say whatever you like in England, so long as you do not say anything to hurt another person, defame him or take away his good name.

This is the meaning of the verse in the Bible (Matthew 7:12): 'Therefore all things whatsoever ye would that men should do to you, do ye even so to them: for this is the law and the prophets.'

It has also meant, in the history of the English people, that although everyone is free—so long as they observe their duties towards the people around them—when power is given to someone to rule over others, that power is only given within limits; and the person who does the ruling must keep within those limits. He is not free to do just as he likes. The Anglo-Saxon kings had to get the advice of their council. This was very well expressed by Bracton, a lawyer in the thirteenth century:

> The king must not be under man but under God and under the
> law, because law makes the king.

The king must obey the law, too. He is not above it. He must
keep God's law and also the law which he, together with his
wise men, give to the people. It would not do to give law to the
people and then disregard it himself. Do you see how this
differs from the Roman law principle, 'What pleases the prince
[meaning king] has the force of law'?

Again and again, in the history of the English nation, this
principle, 'The king must not be under man but under God
and the law', has been re-stated by the judges to remind men
in authority that there is even higher authority above them,
and that they cannot do just as they please.

In the fifteenth century there was civil war in this country,
which we now know as 'the Wars of the Roses'. Civil war is the
worst possible kind of war because it means men of the same
nation fighting and killing each other. During this time Prince
Edward, the son of the king, was sent to France to be safe.
While he was there, the young Prince was instructed by Sir John
Fortescue, who had been Chief Justice under the boy's father,
King Henry VI. The old judge talked to the young prince about
what it meant to be king—what duties he would have to
perform and how to take care of his people. It is all set down in
a famous book called *In Praise of the Laws of England*. Prince
Edward asked questions and Sir John answered them, telling
him of Bracton's famous saying, and how important it was.
Sadly, the young prince was fated not to become king: he died
at the battle of Tewkesbury in 1471 and another Edward, a
ruthless king, took the throne. Fortunately, Chief Justice
Fortescue wrote his book for the benefit of the nation. He
wanted it made known to all the great nobles warring with each
other over the Crown of England that, in the end, they were all
under God and the law. While the battles raged and devastated
the countryside for many years, he did not want it forgotten
that the natural system of government was not the rule and

pleasure of the strongest, but the king and his council
peacefully determining together, and in the light of reason, the
issues facing the people. Chief Justice Fortescue set it down so
that it would not be lost. People read his book and
remembered at a later time, so the principles were not lost.

Less than two hundred years later, another king, James I,
tried to behave as though he were above the law. He wanted to
decide what the law was himself instead of letting the judges do
it. As that meant that the king might have to decide for or
against himself—in cases where some of his own people might
have a claim against him—the judges all said he could not do
it. They went before him in fear and trembling because James
was a vindictive king and they might have been dismissed or
imprisoned in the Tower of London. A man of courage, Chief
Justice Coke, told the king firmly that he was under God and
the law. Some time later King James found a way of getting rid
of Coke, but, nevertheless, the king had to accept the situation.
We are fortunate in having men of courage to speak up for us at
times of crisis for the nation.

Another very great judge, Lord Denning, in recent times
had to restate the principle that the king, and the king's
servants, are all under law. This was a case in which the
Attorney-General, a high officer of state, refused to give to the
court his reasons for acting in a certain way. Lord Denning
said: 'To every subject in this land, no matter how powerful, I
would use Thomas Fuller's words over 300 years ago: "Be you
never so high the law is above you".'

While this love of liberty and respect for duty and the law
were all features of the Anglo-Saxon character, it was King
Alfred who brought them together and founded a nation. He
ruled Wessex (the western part of our country) for thirty years,
from AD 871 to 901. There is an old poem about him:

> There also was Alfred, England's herdsman,
>   England's darling;
> He was king of England, he taught them,
>   All who could hear him,
> How they should lead their lives.

Alfred was a king of England, that was very strong.
He was both king and scholar, he loved well God's work;
He was wise and advised in his talk;
He was the wisest man that was in all England.

And it is a fact that, even today, over one thousand years
later, the memory of this great king is still treasured. We may
not know much about him; but whenever he is mentioned, no-
one speaks ill of him. There are plenty of people to criticise
other kings and statesmen in our history, but not Alfred. It is
well recognised that he gave his life utterly to the service of his
people and the generations to come.

It is a mark of a truly great man that there really is not
anything harmful to say about him. Goodness is all that is
known about him, and he reflects the true nature of mankind.
We are in the presence of Man from whom a nation is able to
spring.

Yet Alfred was human. The stories about him are human
and they make us smile: like the one about his allowing the
bread to burn when an old lady, not knowing he was the king,
left him in charge of her loaves one day. Or the one about him
disguising himself as a minstrel—a wandering singer and
storyteller—in order to get into the camp of his enemy and
find out the secrets of the army.

Throughout his reign, Alfred and his soldiers had to fight
against the Danes, who sailed the North Sea from Denmark, to
invade England. They conquered most of the eastern part of
the country and tried to take over Wessex, but Alfred was too
strong and defeated them. In time of peace as well as war, King
Alfred worked unceasingly to give his people good laws,
education and the firm faith of the Christian religion. So,
although Wessex itself was only the western part of the whole
country, in time this influence spread over the whole of
England, as the nation slowly grew in strength.

You can gain some idea of the quality of Alfred from this
account, written by him, of the task of kingship:

> You know that covetousness and greed for worldly dominion
> never pleased me over much, and that I did not all too greatly

desire this earthly rule, but yet I desired tools and material for the work that I was charged to perform, namely that I might worthily and fittingly steer and rule the dominion that was entrusted to me. You know that no man can reveal any talent or rule and steer any dominion without tools and material. That without which one cannot carry on that craft is the material of every craft. This, then, is a king's material and his tools for ruling with, that he have his land fully manned. He must have men who pray and soldiers and workmen. Lo, you know that without these tools no king can reveal his skill. Also, this is his material, which he must have for those tools—sustenance for those three orders; and their sustenance consists in land to live on, and gifts, and weapons, and food, and ale, and clothes, and whatever else those three orders require. And without these things he cannot hold those tools, nor without those tools do any of the things that he is charged to do. For that reason I desired material to rule that dominion with, that my powers and dominion would not be forgotten and concealed. For every talent and every dominion is soon worn out and silently passed over, if it is without wisdom; because no man can bring forth any craft without wisdom, for whatever is done in folly can never be accounted as a craft. In brief, I desired to live worthily as long as I lived, and to leave after my life, to the men who should come after, my memory in good works.

This is a splendid account of kingship: note how he talks of being entrusted with the kingdom and 'charged to perform' his work, by God. The king needs tools to do his work of building a nation, and the tools are his men, in their three orders—churchmen, soldiers and workmen. Wisdom is what is required of the king to hold the tools and do what he is required to do. And the king hopes to live worthily and to leave good works for the men who come after. King Alfred is both humble and resolute. He knows that authority comes from God, and that it must be exercised, through wisdom, over the men of the kingdom, so that good works are achieved.

Perhaps because of the constant battles with the Danes, the people of Wessex had a sense of unity which the king worked on to mould it into a nation, through law and language and religion. There was a need for books which people could read in their own language: books of the finest quality and great understanding, many of them still in Latin, which was beginning to be forgotten. Alfred himself, despite the wars and his own lengthy illnesses, worked on translating books into Anglo-Saxon, the forerunner of our present-day English language. He asked scholars to come from all over the world to help him in this effort and to establish schools.

The king laid down laws for his people: not laws which he thought up himself, but those which he collected from the scriptures and others which had been tried in practice and found most just. Then, he says, 'I, Alfred, king of the West Saxons, showed these to all my councillors, and they then said that they were all pleased to observe them'. So he did not force these laws on them, but won their consent to his choice.

Of King Alfred, that other great Englishman, Sir Winston Churchill, has written:

> We discern across the centuries a commanding and versatile intelligence, wielding with equal force the sword of war and of justice; using in defence arms and policy; cherishing religion, learning and art in the midst of adversity and danger; welding together a nation, and seeking always across the feuds and hatreds of the age a peace which would smile upon the land.

3

Government

Self rides in the chariot of the body, intellect the firm-footed charioteer, discursive mind the reins.

Senses are the horses, objects of desire the roads. When Self is joined to body, mind, sense, none but He enjoys.

When a man lack steadiness, unable to control his mind, his senses are unmanageable horses.

But if he control his mind, a steady man, they are manageable horses.—*Katha Upanishad*

The best kind of government is self-government. We will often hear this term 'self-government' used, particularly about a state or country which has been ruled from outside, by another state, and has now achieved its independence and can choose its own rulers. In a way, it has grown up; and, like children who grow up, it naturally wants to do things for itself and not at the dictates of parents.

Socrates said that, if you were looking for justice, you might find it in the state as well as in the individual person, but it might be larger and easier to see in the workings of the state. Each of us has a 'government', which is mind, telling us what is right and best for us to do, and arranging for the body to do it. To the extent that we obey, and perform our duty towards others, there is very little need for outside authorities, like policemen and judges and parliaments, to tell us what to do. But if we act only in our own narrow interests, forgetting the duties to others, then we really have not grown up yet and must expect to be directed from outside.

What governs how we behave?

The passage at the head of this chapter comes from a very old scripture. It describes the body as a chariot being drawn by horses, the senses: and that is exactly how it feels, when we see something or smell something that we want and the body hastens towards it. The charioteer is intellect: and by that the ancients meant the part of the mind which chooses between right and wrong, true and false. The passenger in the chariot, in the body—whether it is the body of an individual or of the nation—is called 'the Self'. What is meant by 'the Self'?

It is what we call the soul, or divine spirit, in each man. We take it with us wherever we go, and whatever we do; we never lose it and it outlasts the body. But, more than that, everything comes from the Self: all our desires and thoughts and activities start from that still centre. It is the quiet, observant passenger: yet, at the same time, it is the powerhouse for all energy and all activity. The Self is going on a journey in the body, and the purpose, the aim, of the journey is to make truth evident in creation.

What a marvellous analogy it all is, the chariot of the body being taken along the roads of life, with the charioteer of intellect to direct the horses: and all for the sake of the passenger, without whom the whole lot would not exist!

It is most important that we get a sense of this: all power, all energy, all activity come ultimately from God. Without Him, we could not do or say anything. We are entirely dependent on the Creator and on the still, quiet centre which He has placed in every man. From that stillness and quietness come all authority and all law.

There is a story in the Bible of a Roman centurion who came to Jesus to ask Him to heal his servant who was very ill. Jesus said:

> I will come and heal him.
> The centurion answered and said, Lord, I am not worthy that thou shouldest come under my roof: but speak the word only, and my servant shall be healed.
> For I am a man under authority, having soldiers under me: and I say to this man, Go, and he goeth; and to another, Come, and he cometh; and to my servant, Do this, and he doeth it.

Jesus marvelled at the centurion's faith; and gave the word and the servant was healed. The story shows that the centurion knew that all things happen under the authority of God, and that Jesus, who was the Son of God, merely had to command for events to follow. But the centurion himself could call on the same power of God to get soldiers in the army to do his bidding. He had to utter the right words and men would come and go.

We are all given this great power to do things. It happens all the time, in the simplest ways. If you raise your hand, for example, there is something in the mind which gives the order and the sinews and muscles obey: but where did the action start from and what effect does it have afterwards? We see only part of it. You might raise your hand to ward off a blow: but where did the desire to hit you come from and where does it go afterwards? All that we can say is that the action appears out of stillness; we see it take place and then it disappears into stillness again, just like the words we use in a sentence.

Alexander Pope wrote a poem called 'Essay on Man' in 1733. In it he said:

All Nature is but art unknown to thee;
All chance, direction, which thou can'st not see;
All discord, harmony not understood;
All partial evil, universal good;
And spite of pride, in erring reason's spite,
One truth is clear, whatsoever is, is right.

So here is another way of looking at those words 'self-government', in which it really does become the best kind of government. That is, to remember the Self, the presence of God in each of us, and to behave always with the knowledge that we have a most precious passenger in the chariot of the body. The Self is always there, even if we take Him for a bumpy ride, and even if we wreck the chariot by allowing the horses to get out of control. The Self will not be affected. But if the charioteer, the reasoning part of mind, is quiet and still and listens, the Self governs and will tell him what to do and which roads to take.

In the chariot of the nation there has to be someone firm-footed, like the charioteer, capable of remaining quiet and still and yet giving the right directions. This is known, in the government of a nation, as the 'sovereign'. With us the sovereign is the Queen in Parliament.

There cannot be two sovereigns: you cannot have two charioteers driving at the same time. One has to decide which way is right for the chariot to go. As we saw in the previous chapter, a time of civil war is disastrous for a nation, because it becomes divided, trying to serve two masters. This it cannot do, if it is to remain one nation.

The Queen is the still point of government. She is always on duty, always watchful over the nation. She never appears to act, and yet she acts all the time. The position she holds, which is described as 'majesty', requires absolute service and dedication from her. People sometimes talk of her as though she were just a figurehead: someone who is exalted and praised and admired but has very little to do with the actual running of the country. Nothing could be further from the truth. As we shall see when we come to consider the part the Queen plays, she is constantly informed about what is going on; and all government activity comes under her scrutiny. When people say that the Queen nowadays has no power to act, it is because they do not understand that activities can only be controlled when they are watched from stillness. The Upanishad tell us, 'When a man lack steadiness, unable to control his mind, his senses are unmanageable horses'. The Queen observes all that goes on from quietness; and hence the government of the nation does not get out of hand.

Imagine what it would be like if the charioteer got excited and panic-stricken when the horses started to go fast! How would the horses be controlled?

All power and authority in the state are derived from the Queen. You may have seen envelopes with the letters 'O.H.M.S.' on them—they signify 'On Her Majesty's Service', which means that the envelopes contain documents or orders of state. The Queen's Ministers are 'Ministers of the Crown', that is, 'servants of the Crown'. Their function is to serve the needs of the nation. Service is of utmost importance throughout the nation: and service is always from the strong to the weak. The Queen, for example, serves everyone. It is the Queen in Parliament who is sovereign.

Parliament is very old. It comes from the councils of those old Anglo-Saxon kings. In those days it was called 'witenagemot', which means assembly of the wise. If you look at that word, you can see in it our word 'wit' which meant wise (and not funny, as it has come to mean today). And also 'mot' or 'moot', which is still a word we use sometimes to describe an assembly of people. 'Parliament' comes from a French word, *parler*, meaning 'to speak', and indicates how we are ruled by speech. We are governed by words. Everything we do or see or think about has to be expressed in words: and so at the highest level in the nation Parliament uses words to direct us.

These words are shaped into 'Acts of Parliament'. These Acts tell us what we have to do. There are Acts to tell us how to drive on the roads; how to buy and sell goods; what will happen if we steal, and so on. There are massive books containing all these Acts, and lawyers to sort through them. Perhaps, today, there are altogether too many Acts of Parliament: but if there are, it only means that we have forgoten ourselves and our duties to others, and need to be reminded of them—sometimes forcibly.

The three parts of Parliament, the Queen, the House of Lords and the House of Commons have all to agree for an Act to be passed into law. There is an old form of words which precedes each Act:

> Be it enacted by the Queen's most Excellent Majesty, by and with the advice and consent of the Lords Spiritual and Temporal, and Commons, in this present Parliament assembled, and by the authority of the same. . .

That is an old and very exact description of sovereignty and it still works in the nation today. Notice that it does not say that the Queen and her Ministers will *do* anything: only that they will *carry out* whatever is expressed in the Act itself. It recognises a sequence of events and that we are all instruments of the Creator. If the 'advice and consent' of the Lords and Commons are thoughtfully given, then events will take the right path for the good of the nation. In the analogy of the chariot, the horses will be steered along the right road.

We show overleaf an example of the title-page of an Act of Parliament. At the top you see the Queen's name; below it the Royal coat-of-arms; then the title of the particular Act and the year and chapter number. The chapter number is the place that this Act will have when, at the end of the year, all the Acts which have received Royal Assent are bound together in a book. Underneath is what is called the 'preamble', which pretty well describes itself: a 'walking about' so that you get a sense of what the Act is all about before you go for a long excursion into the text. After that is the date on which the vital third factor in the process of government, the Queen, gave her assent to the Act; and then the enacting formula which we discussed above.

Both the House of Lords and the House of Commons have to give their 'advice and consent'. The House of Lords is, with the Queen, the oldest part of government, coming from the councils of the elders which attended the Anglo-Saxon kings. There are Lords Spiritual (the bishops of the church); Lords Temporal (men and women who represent the great land-owning families of the kingdom; and also, today, life peers, who have given distinguished service to the nation); and the most senior judges. Thus the great institutions of the nation are represented in the House of Lords: the Church, the law, landowners, the universities, commerce and trade unions. The qualities which one expects from the Lords are wisdom and stability. They do not usually start an Act of Parliament but they are there to give wise deliberation and to suggest changes and improvements.

Those responsible for the day-to-day administration of the nation's affairs are the Prime Minister and the Ministers sitting in the House of Commons. They are ordinary Members of Parliament first, elected like all the other Members by the people, and then, secondly, Ministers of the Crown. Members of Parliament are elected to represent areas of the country, called 'constituencies', and they are referred to as the 'Honourable Member for Hereford' or Croydon South or

Animals Act 1971   c. **22**

ELIZABETH II

1971 CHAPTER 22

An Act to make provision with respect to civil liability for damage done by animals and with respect to the protection of livestock from dogs; and for purposes connected with those matters.   [12th May 1971]

BE IT ENACTED by the Queen's most Excellent Majesty, by and with the advice and consent of the Lords Spiritual and Temporal, and Commons, in this present Parliament assembled, and by the authority of the same, as follows:—

Strict liability for damage done by animals

1.—(1) The provisions of sections 2 to 5 of this Act replace—

> (a) the rules of the common law imposing a strict liability in tort for damage done by an animal on the ground that the animal is regarded as ferae naturae or that its vicious or mischievous propensities are known or presumed to be known;

> (b) subsections (1) and (2) of section 1 of the Dogs Act 1906 as amended by the Dogs (Amendment) Act 1928 (injury to cattle or poultry); and

> (c) the rules of the common law imposing a liability for cattle trespass.

New provisions as to strict liability for damage done by animals.

1906 c. 32.
1928 c. 21.

(2) Expressions used in those sections shall be interpreted in accordance with the provisions of section 6 (as well as those of section 11) of this Act.

2.—(1) Where any damage is caused by an animal which belongs to a dangerous species, any person who is a keeper of the animal is liable for the damage, except as otherwise provided by this Act.

Liability for damage done by dangerous animals.

whatever. So they come into Parliament to represent the people living in each area; but, of course, once there they are bound to debate the national interest.

The House of Commons is very much the 'discursive mind', 'the reins', mentioned in the Upanishad. The reins control the horses; they are held by the firm-footed charioteer; and they give direction. But they also give information about the horses: they tell the driver what the horses are feeling, what they want to do and where they are likely to go if not restrained. This 'discursive mind' is called intelligence: that is, it tells the higher part of mind, the intellect, what exactly is going on in the body and all around it. So it is connected with the senses, which usually conduct the body through life, as the horses pull the chariot.

The House of Commons is altogether a more excitable place than the Lords. Members of Parliament do things at times which their Lordships probably would not think of doing. In the long history of the Commons there are some very amusing scenes:

> 16 July, 1610–Affirmed by Mr. Speaker, that Sir E. Herbert put not off his hat to him, but put out his tongue, and popped his mouth with his finger, in scorn;
> that Mr. T.T., in a loud and violent manner, and, contrary to the usage of Parliament, standing near the Speaker's Chair, cried 'Baw' in the Speaker's ear, to the great terror and affrightment of the Speaker and of the members of the House.

Proceedings in the House have become more orderly since those days; but it is because the Speaker of the House has, now, considerable powers to keep things from getting out of hand. The rules are much more strict than in the House of Lords. This is because the Commons are 'the great debate of the nation': where the feelings and opinions of the time are aired. Opinions are ideas we have, true or false, about what is happening. And in the debates of the House of Commons you will find reflected all the opinions that people have and the way they feel about things and what they want to do about them.

These opinions and feelings are the 'objects of sense', the roads which the horses have to follow, in the Upanishad.

So, of course, from time to time the discussion becomes heated. But the Speaker of the House, like the Queen, watches over it all from a still centre, and holds the House. Then it is possible for reason to enter and for Members to listen to reasonable speech. They have, on the table of the House, the mace which is always borne before the Speaker when he comes in, and then placed in brackets to indicate that the Commons are in session. The mace was a battle-club in the days when knights in armour used to take swings at each other. Now, in the old Sanskrit literature, reason was described as a club: a weapon with which to hit false ideas on the head. Members of Parliament, therefore, have the symbol of reason before them whenever they rise to express the ideas of the time.

Just as the reins are sensitive to what is happening to the horses, so the Commons are sensitive to all the opinions and beliefs of the people. They discuss them, and out of the discussion arise the plans and proposals for what to do. But who gives the people those opinions and beliefs in the first place?

The Prime Minister and Ministers would like to think that it is *they* who think of the ideas which would benefit the people; and that the 'sense objects', the roads which the country is going to take, are what *they* think the people would want. When elections come along you will hear many fine promises of things that Members of Parliament will do, if they get elected, which will make life better for the people. But, often enough, what people want has already been established for them by writers and artists and thinkers quite outside the Houses of Parliament.

It is what we read and learn when we go to school that is of great importance here. If you go on to university then it is likely that the books you read there, and the ideas you pick up, will govern the rest of your life. And if you write about those ideas and beliefs, and speak about them, they will have their effect on many, many people who do not think for themselves.

In the Upanishad it speaks of the 'objects of desire' being

the roads down which the horses, the senses, will travel. The senses often dominate the way we live. Most people live their lives by their senses and do not bother with reading the works of great men, or thinking for themselves. Others must do it for them and then put their understanding in such a way that everyone else can easily follow. For example, in the days when most men and women were not trained to read, the lessons of the Bible were laid out for them in the stained-glass windows of the churches. Have a look some time at these magnificent pictures, in stained glass. Just consider the intelligence and the love of the men who painted and put those windows there, for the benefit of those who could not read the words of the Bible.

It is a very great power, this use of words and pictures to rule men. And it is a power which can be used for good or evil. The same intelligence and the same skills are needed for drawing pictures filled with violence and hate, which make men do evil things, as are required to paint pictures which enrich men's lives.

Often, therefore, it seems that the artists and writers and thinkers have made roads for us which it is impossible not to follow. Fortunately, all the very greatest of them work from a high level of goodness. Their words and music and pictures shine for us and outlast their inferiors.

So government must, in the first place, ensure that education is well done. You will remember that King Alfred made this his first concern, even when he was much troubled by wars and the problems of state. He brought together as many fine scholars as he could; and he was at pains to translate the best available books into the English language, so that more people had access to them.

Government holds the reins and checks the impulse of the horses if they are galloping down a road towards their own destruction. The roads are the sense objects which attract us; but often there are crossroads where several paths meet, and then a choice has to be made, whether to go down one towards disaster or down another towards Man's true happiness. These roads are made of ideas. Many times a road which looks straight and broad and promising, in fact turns out to lead to trouble; whereas another one looks difficult and narrow and yet is the right one to take. The firm-footed charioteer has to make the choice.

Not many years ago this country was very reluctant to go to war against evil forces which had built themselves up in Germany and which threatened goodness everywhere. It was a grim path to have to take because it meant misery and bloodshed. And there were men in government who wanted peace above all else—but it was the kind of peace that would have meant even greater suffering and tyranny. So the choice was made, to go to war, to save humanity. And the people, given the inspiration of the man who became their Prime Minister, Sir Winston Churchill, did go to war and did save civilisation. But first they listened to the words of their King, King George VI, as he spoke to them over the radio on a Sunday evening in September 1939. Part of what he said was this:

> For the sake of all that we ourselves hold dear, and of the world's order and peace, it is unthinkable that we should refuse to meet the challenge.
>
> It is to this high purpose that I now call my people at home and my peoples across the seas, who will make our cause their own. I ask them to stand calm and firm and united in this time of trial.
>
> The task will be hard. There may be dark days ahead, and war can no longer be confined to the battlefield. But we can only do the right as we see the right, and reverently commit our cause to God.
>
> If one and all we keep resolutely faithful to it, ready for whatever service or sacrifice it may demand, then, with God's help, we shall prevail.
>
> May He bless and keep us all.

This is a good illustration of the firm-footed charioteer, guiding the horses of the nation, and, at the same time, being aware fully of God's presence.

4

Coronation

> And the prince shall pray that the providence of God which has raised him to rule so great an empire be pleased to give him justice, piety and wisdom; justice to his subjects, piety towards God, wisdom in the government of his kingdom, that softened by no favour, disturbed by no enemies, seduced by no lust, and hampered by no other passion, he may walk with firm foot in the paths of these virtues.—*Liber Regalis* (fourteenth century)

We are ruled by the Queen in Parliament. That again tells us something about the purpose and direction of government: because the word 'rule' means going in a straight line. The ruler we use to draw lines with would not be much good if it were bent or crooked. It might take a pencil along a path between two points, but it certainly would not be 'the shortest distance between two points', which is the definition of a straight line. We could go very much astray before we reached the second point if we could not rely on the ruler being straight; and all other calculations, based on that line, would be wrong.

Notice that we have used the one word 'ruler' both to denote a simple piece of wood which has been cut and shaped to guide a pencil in a straight line; and also to denote the highest office of state. So that indicates that persons who occupy the highest offices of state are instruments, too, just like the piece of wood. Their function is to guide us along a straight line. This straight line, according to Plato, is the Will of God.

You will remember that we talked about this in Chapter 3: we saw that the Self or Soul goes on a journey in the chariot of the body and, if the road is the right one, eventually the Self arrives home, which is its own essential bliss, or happiness.

All this is of the greatest importance in the conduct of the affairs of the nation, because the nation is a greater body incorporating all the lesser bodies, including you and me. It is therefore essential that the nation be guided along the path of rectitude, which is another word to do with straightness. Rectitude also means uprightness: the natural way for a man to walk, bearing himself like a man and remembering all the time the divinity within him. To stray from that path always brings misery, poverty, unhappiness. Thus our rulers should always be men and women who set an example that we can follow.

In setting that example, of course, they are serving us. The idea of service is, today, not a very popular one. People mistakenly think that serving others is somehow beneath them: that the ideal state of affairs would be where everyone could do what they liked for themselves, without having to rely on anyone else. It is plainly nonsense, yet it is an old idea and a very strong one. Jesus said:

> . . . whosoever will be great among you, let him be your minister;
> And whosoever will be chief among you, let him be your servant;
> Even as the Son of man came not to be ministered unto, but to minister and to give his life a ransom for many.

Her Majesty Queen Elizabeth II serves us all, both as head of State and head of the Church, at the highest level in the nation. Her life is one continuous act of service, and always has been. When she was twenty-one, and still a Royal Princess, she made a radio broadcast in which she said:

> I declare before you all that my whole life, whether it be long or short, shall be devoted to your service and the service of our great Imperial Commonwealth to which we all belong. But I shall not have strength to carry out this resolution unless you join in it with me, as I now invite you to do; I know that your support will be unfailingly given. God bless all of you who are willing to share it.

When she became Queen, her act of service to her people was dedicated to God in the holy and mysterious form of coronation, which means 'crowning'. This splendid occasion took place in Westminster Abbey, as it has done for hundreds of years. If you go to the Abbey you can see the Coronation Chair which is old and battered and scored with people's initials! It is called 'King Edward's Chair', made by order of King Edward I to hold the 'Stone of Destiny' captured from the Scots in 1296. This stone was by legend supposed to be the pillow on which Jacob, the father of another and very old nation, the Israelites, slept.

And, of course, you should go to the Tower of London, to see all the magnificent robes and crown jewels which are worn at a coronation. The Tower is a royal palace and fortress commanding the approaches to London along the river. To see the crown jewels you have to go underground into a dim, steel-bound vault, for the jewels are very precious and have to be protected. Only once has anyone managed to steal them: in 1671 when a certain Captain Blood attacked the Keeper of the Jewels. However, he did not get far: the Keeper's son raised the alarm and Blood was captured.

London is truly the capital of a nation, for 'capital' means 'head'. Here, close together, you will find the buildings which house the institutions that go to make up the headship of the nation. First there is Westminster Abbey where the spirit and the body of the nation come together, especially at coronation-time, in dedication and holy communion. Then, close by, is the Palace of Westminster where Parliament sits; and, only just the other side of St James's Park, Buckingham Palace, the London home of the Queen. Further along the river are the Royal Courts of Justice where, in the 'Queen's Bench', it is said the Queen sits giving law—only today it is done by the Queen's judges, the Justices of the Queen's Bench in their scarlet robes. Beyond the law courts lies the City, the oldest part of London, where the merchants and bankers transact their business. It is all a rich panorama for anyone with eyes to see the texture of a living nation. Only one part of government, the oldest and wisest universities, Oxford and Cambridge, where the ideas that govern a nation are properly reflected on and studied, are placed at some distance from the capital city. That is right, too, for they need to be located in quiet places, where the mind can rest, away from the hustle and bustle of everyday affairs.

Here, then, in the Abbey of Westminster, the Queen is crowned. She enters in procession, wearing crimson velvet robes, and before her are carried the two-handed Sword of State and the Swords of Justice and Mercy. Justice is represented by a sword because anyone who wrongs the state is liable to be punished; but the Sword of Mercy has a lovely name, 'Curtana', and its blade is broken about six inches from the point, leaving a flat, blunt end, the ancient symbol representing mercy. The name Curtana comes from 'Courtain', the sword of Ogier the Dane, an eighth-century warrior. He was supposed to have drawn Courtain against an Emperor's son in revenge for the killing of his own son, but drew back when a voice from Heaven called upon him to show mercy. This quality of mercy is something the Queen possesses and can use, when need be, to reward someone, which is its original meaning. We tend to think of mercy as something which is given to someone to excuse them from what seems to be their rightful punishment: but it is not that, it really is a reward for showing signs of becoming a better man and citizen.

The Queen is then presented to the people by the Archbishop, turning and facing the four points, East, South, West and North and at every one of them saying:

> Sirs, I here present unto you Queen Elizabeth, your undoubted Queen: Wherefore all you who are come this day to do your homage and service, Are you willing to do the same?

And the people in the Abbey cry out, 'God save Queen Elizabeth'. And the trumpets sound.

This part of the Coronation Service is called the Recognition, or Election by the People. But it is somewhat different from what we have come to suppose is election, which means several people offering themselves for membership, say, of the House of Commons, and the voters having to choose between them. The one who gets the highest number of 'votes' is said to be elected. But there was no choosing our Queen: as the eldest daughter of the last king, King George VI, who had no son to follow him, Queen Elizabeth naturally became monarch on the death of her father.

The word 'vote' originally meant 'vow': this meaning is closer to what happens in the Abbey when the Archbishop presents the Queen. By their shout of acclamation the people are giving their solemn promise, their vow, to follow the leadership of the Queen and to support her. It was, you remember, what she asked for in her radio broadcast (see page 30). In this sense voting becomes a much more positive thing—requiring constant loyalty from the people to the Queen—than merely marking a cross on a piece of paper to elect someone a member of Parliament.

The Queen is then required to make an oath in return. She promises to govern her peoples 'according to their respective laws and customs'. Here she pledges herself not to try to be greater than the law or to take it in her own hands for selfish purposes: which is a reminder of the famous words of Bracton, 'The king must not be under man but under God and under the law, because law makes the king.' She promises to 'cause Law and Justice, in Mercy, to be executed in all [her] judgments'. Of course, the judgments will be made by her judges: but they will, if they are good judges, be constantly aware of the Queen's presence in the work they do, and they, in turn, will make oath to the Queen when they are appointed judges. Then the Archbishop asks her whether she will, to the utmost of her power, maintain the Laws of God and the true profession of the Gospel, and the Church of England of which she is now the head. She answers: 'All this I promise to do.'

By this oath the Queen accepts responsibility for government; for the administration of the law; and for the church. It is no light burden. And when the people shout 'God save Queen Elizabeth' they are really asking for her preservation and strength to undertake this burden for them.

The strength comes with the next part of the coronation service which is to do with the consecration of the Queen. Consecration means 'to make sacred'. The office of Queen is a most holy one, linking the nation with the Creator. This is why so many people, across the world, who have other forms of government and do not acknowledge the Queen as their head of state, yet find it an awe-inspiring experience to meet her. She is one ruler who is consecrated to the task: that is, the English nation wants, at its head, someone who is aware of the religious significance of the nation's life and purpose.

Edmund Burke, the eighteenth-century statesman, said: 'This consecration is made, that all who administer in the government of men, in which they stand in the person of God himself, should have high and worthy notions of their function and destination.'

So the Archbishop, having anointed the Queen with holy oil, says this:

> Our Lord Jesus Christ, the Son of God, who by his Father was anointed with the Oil of gladness above his fellows, by his holy Anointing pour down upon your Head and Heart the blessing of the Holy Ghost, and prosper the works of your Hands: that by the assistance of his heavenly grace you may preserve the people committed to your charge in wealth, peace, and godliness; and after a long and glorious course of ruling a temporal kingdom wisely, justly, and religiously, you may at last be made partaker of an eternal kingdom, through Jesus Christ our Lord.

This is followed by the investment of the Queen with the royal robes and ornaments, ending with the crowning. She first puts on the white 'Colobium Sindonis' and then the Supertunica or Close Pall, a sleeved robe of cloth of gold lined with crimson silk, together with the girdle or sword belt. The Golden Spurs, which signify knighthood, are brought from the altar and touched by the Queen. The Jewelled State Sword is put into the right hand of the Queen. The Archbishop says:

> With this sword do justice, stop the growth of iniquity, protect the holy Church of God, help and defend widows and orphans, restore the things that are gone to decay, maintain the things that are restored, punish and reform what is amiss, and confirm what is in good order. . .

The investing with the Armills, or 'bracelets of sincerity and wisdom', and the Robe Royal or Pall of cloth of gold, with the Stole Royal, follows. The Sovereign has now received all the royal vestments and the delivery of the rest of the ornaments

begins. First comes the Orb. As the Archbishop places it in the
Queen's right hand he says: 'And when you see this Orb thus
set under the Cross, remember that the whole world is subject
to the Power and Empire of Christ our Redeemer.'

Next comes the Coronation Ring, 'the ensign of kingly
dignity'. This is followed by investiture with the Sceptres. The
Sceptre with the Cross, signifying 'kingly power and justice', is
set in the Queen's right hand and the Sceptre with the Dove,
'the rod of equity and mercy', in the left. The Archbishop says:

> Receive the Rod of equity and mercy: and God, from whom all
> holy desires, all good counsels, and all just works do proceed,
> direct and assist you in the administration and exercise of all
> those powers which he hath given you. Be so merciful that you
> be not too remiss; so execute justice that you forget not mercy.
> Punish the wicked, protect and cherish the just, and lead your
> people in the way wherein they should go.

Now comes the supreme moment when the Archbishop
raises the glittering St Edward's Crown and places it on the
Queen's head. As he does so the people in the Abbey cry out,
'God save the Queen'. The princes and princesses and the
nobles all, as one, raise their coronets and put them on, the
trumpets sound and at the Tower of London the great guns
boom out their salute.

Then the Queen receives the homage of her nobles. Her
own family first and then the most senior of the various orders,
dukes, marquesses, earls, viscounts and barons come forward
one by one and, kneeling, say:

> I do become your liege man of life and limb, and of earthly
> worship; and faith and truth I will bear unto you, to live and
> die, against all manner of folks. So help me God.

The word 'homage' is interesting. It comes from two Latin
words, *homo*, meaning 'man' and *age*, meaning 'belonging to'.
So this vow which is given is that which belongs to a man. It is a
man's work to support and serve the King or Queen. The old
orders of nobility are based on the kinds of service men are

capable of giving to their nation: very great service at the top
and so on down the scale. Great figures of the past, men like
Marlborough and Wellington, who fought and won battles for
the nation, were honoured with dukedoms. And the families
they established, their sons and their sons' sons, have had this
standard to live up to and to be trained in. Sir Winston
Churchill, for example, one of the greatest prime ministers we
have had, was a descendant of the first Duke of Marlborough.

'When the Homage is ended', says the book of the
coronation service, 'the drums shall beat, and the trumpets
sound, and all the people shout, crying out:

God Save Queen Elizabeth
Long live Queen Elizabeth
May the Queen live for ever.'

It is no wonder that those who have been close to kings and
queens have described a kind of marvellous light, a spiritual
radiance, emanating from them during the splendid ceremony
of coronation.

So the form and shape of the coronation service we have just
been describing may be summarised as follows:

(1) The Queen is accepted by the people at THE RECOG-
NITION.
(2) In taking THE OATH, the Queen swears to govern by the
Nation's laws.
(3) At the ANOINTING, the Queen receives a special Blessing
for her life and work.
(4) THE INVESTING and ENTHRONING are the outward
and visible signs of the Queen's taking up her office.

But the ceremony, splendid and holy as it is, also has its
humorous and human side. King George VI, our present
Queen's father, noted in his diary after his own coronation:

I had two Bishops, Durham and Bath and Wells, one on either
side to support me and to hold the form of service for me to
follow. When this great moment came neither Bishop could
find the words, so the Archbishop held his book down for me

to read, but, horror of horrors, his thumb covered the words of the Oath.

My Lord Great Chamberlain was supposed to dress me but I found his hands fumbled and shook so I had to fix the belt of the sword myself. As it was, he nearly put the hilt of the sword under my chin trying to attach it to the belt. . .

As I turned after leaving the Coronation Chair I was brought up all standing, owing to one of the Bishops treading on my robe. I had to tell him to get off it pretty sharply as I nearly fell down.

5

What the Queen does

> The Supreme EXECUTIVE Power of this Kingdom is lodged
> in a single Person; the KING or QUEEN.—*Blackstone*

The statement by Sir William Blackstone which heads this
chapter is of great importance in our system of government.
He speaks of the 'supreme executive power', which means
that, at the highest level, the nation can only act through the
Queen. She gives power to act.

We saw that we are ruled by the Queen in Parliament. And
an 'Act of Parliament' is a course of action which is agreed on
by the House of Commons, the House of Lords and the
Queen. But only one of those has the power to put the words of
the Act of Parliament into effect: it is the Queen.

Thus, once again, she serves the whole nation, for the
Queen who causes things to be done is obedient to the Queen
in Parliament which decides on that course of action. The old
words are still very true: 'Be it enacted by the Queen's most
Excellent Majesty, by and with the advice and consent of the
Lords Spiritual and Temporal, and Commons, in this present
Parliament assembled, and by the authority of the same, as
follows. . .'

Of course, the Queen does not run around the country
doing things. Everything is done in her name. She has a Prime
Minister and Ministers to direct activities; she has generals to
command the army; her judges are the Queen's Judges; and
the postmen who come round deliver the 'Royal Mail'. What,
then, is the power that she has and gives which makes all this
activity possible?

We are reminded of the story of the chariot: 'Self rides in the
chariot of the body, intellect the firm-footed charioteer. . .' All
action comes from the Self; and yet the Self is utterly still. It is
an ever-watchful passenger in the chariot.

One step away is the driver, the firm-footed charioteer, constantly aware of the presence of the Self, or Soul. The charioteer has tremendous power over the horses, yet it is exercised quietly, gently, firmly, just by a touch of the reins. So it is with the Queen. She links the nation with the Creator. She is required to be ever-watchful and alert to see that things do not go wrong. Occasionally she may have to give a touch of the reins to ensure that the people are heading in the right direction. No-one knows the full extent of the powers of the Queen because they come from the limitless Creator. That is why we do not have what is called a 'written' constitution—a document which sets down in words what the Queen can and cannot do. The wisdom of our forefathers saw that it would be impossible to tell what events a future King or Queen would have to meet.

The editor of *The Times* once wrote about King George VI:

> Ministers come and go, but the King remains, always at the centre of public affairs, always participating vigilantly in the work of government from a standpoint detached from any consideration but the welfare of his peoples as a whole. He is the continuous element in the constitution. . .

We call the powers that the Queen has, but which lie hidden, her 'prerogative'. Blackstone describes it thus:

> By the word prerogative we usually understand that special pre-eminence, which the king hath, over and above all other persons, and out of the ordinary course of the common law, in right of his regal dignity. It signifies . . . [from *prae* and *rogo*] something that is required or demanded before, or in preference to, all others.

A brilliant journalist of the last century, Walter Bagehot, wrote a lively account of the English constitution. In it he said:

> . . . it would very much surprise people if they were only told how many things the Queen could do without consulting Parliament. . . Not to mention other things, she could disband the army; . . . she could dismiss all the officers, from the General Commanding-in-chief downwards; she could dismiss all the sailors, too; she could sell off all our ships of war and all

our naval stores. . . She could make every citizen in the United Kingdom, male or female, a peer; she could make every parish in the United Kingdom a 'University'; she could dismiss most of the civil servants; she could pardon all offenders. In a word, the Queen could by prerogative upset all the action of civil government within the government, could disgrace the nation by a bad war or peace, and could, by disbanding our forces, whether land or sea, leave us defenceless against foreign nations.

The author goes on to ask, 'Why do we not fear that she would do this?' The answer is that normally the Queen would not use her great powers without consulting the Prime Minister and his colleagues in the cabinet. They, in turn, are Members of Parliament and must explain themselves to all the other Members sitting in the House of Commons. So it is not likely that the prerogative would be used unless the nation, through its representatives, wanted it to be.

The great secret here is to understand that such great powers exist, even if they are hardly ever used. It is that which is not defined, not limited, which is powerful. Just as the ordinary citizen in this country is allowed to do and think and say whatever he likes so long as it does not hurt another, so the Queen has the freedom and the strength to do what she likes, provided—and this is all-important—she never uses that power to do wrong. She has only the power to do right.

This word 'right' needs to be understood. Far too many people today talk about their 'rights' as though they had something due to them. This is very selfish. In fact, 'right' means straight, correct, true, just, proper. It means behaving naturally; doing what is necessary and required by the events in which we find ourselves. In this sense 'doing right' is the same as 'duty', or what is due to someone else. If we only realised that serving others is the same as serving one's self, we would not have people crying out that they lack 'rights'.

Bagehot also says that, in her dealings with her Prime Minister and other Ministers, the Queen ought always to be consulted about the affairs of state: and then she can do two things—she can encourage and she can warn. He says that these powers, that is, to encourage and to warn, are all she needs. If a Prime Minister comes to her with an idea for the good of the people, the Queen can say, 'Well, I have more experience than you: I have seen this idea tried before and it failed. It could be made better by doing so-and-so. If you go ahead and do it as you propose, then I warn you that such-and-such will happen.' It might be that the Prime Minister would want to do it his way, even after the Queen's warning; but, says Bagehot, 'his mind would be troubled'. In fact, a sensible Prime Minister would take very much into account what his monarch told him, and rarely, if ever, would go against the Queen's wishes.

This is an example of the Queen watching over the affairs of her peoples and exercising a moderating and restraining influence over what is done for the sake of their own best interests. The Royal Family are trained to accept this great responsibility. That is why the Crown is inherited; why Prince Charles, or if he dies, Prince William, will assume the high position of King. From very early on in their lives, the young princes and princesses are made aware that they must put the nation before their own likes and dislikes, wants and desires. There is a story about the present Queen that when she was a small child she was taken by her grandmother, Queen Mary, to a concert. She was wriggling in her chair and the old Queen asked her whether she wanted to go home. The little princess said she could not possibly go because there were a lot of people waiting to see her when she departed, after the concert. Immediately Queen Mary ordered a lady-in-waiting to take Princess Elizabeth home, by a back door where she would not be seen. It would not do for the princess to think that the people waiting outside existed for her own personal delight. Rather, the other way round. And, indeed, Her Majesty Queen Elizabeth II has always shown total dedication to the service of the nation.

When the Queen had been twenty-five years on the throne, in 1977, there was a great service of thanksgiving to God, in St Paul's Cathedral. Afterwards the Queen walked through the streets of the City of London; and everywhere she was met with admiration and with love. This is the result of total dedication to the service of others: it brings with it love and a sense of unity.

Wherever the Queen goes, she is always on call. Even when she goes on holiday, to Balmoral or Sandringham, the red boxes containing state papers are brought to her daily, and she must study them, sign the necessary orders and write her comments. The Prime Minister goes to see her weekly; and there have been Prime Ministers who have gone away somewhat ashamed of themselves because they have not done their homework properly, and have been told by the Queen about things which have happened that they should have remembered.

There are a great many public appearances. There are tours of Commonwealth and foreign countries overseas. The Queen is Head of the Commonwealth. This used to be called the 'British Empire' and now consists of a family of states which still recognise the Queen of England as their head. When we talked about nation, you remember, we said that the distinguishing features of a nation are its own law, language and religion. In this sense there is still very much an Anglo-Saxon nation spread throughout the world today: for the states which belong to the Commonwealth by and large speak English, keep to the common law tradition, and have Christian beliefs. So the Queen is not only Queen of the United Kingdom of Great Britain and Northern Ireland but also of Canada, Australia, New Zealand, The Bahamas, Mauritius, Fiji, Barbados, Jamaica, Grenada and Papua New Guinea. She is not only Head of this great family but also Head of State in each; and when she goes to Canada, for example, she is Queen of Canada.

When she was crowned Queen in London, in 1953, her coronation was celebrated by about a quarter of the total of mankind then living—a huge figure, something like 650 millions. To all of them she represents an important link between the everyday life and what lies behind the mystery of government; between the spirit of mankind and the nation.

It does not even stop there. Once the great and powerful

United States of America were colonies of this country—that is, men from the British Isles went to the continent of America and started new states, 'provinces', as they were called. These all owed allegiance to the Crown of England: but, in large part due to the bad government of the then King and his ministers, they broke away in the eighteenth century and formed their own society. Nevertheless they continued to speak the English language, to live under the common law and to share the religious beliefs of the mother country.

And, today, many, many Americans come every year to the British Isles to spend their holidays here. They do so to visit and enjoy many of the institutions and ceremonies which we, who live here, rather take for granted. London is one of the few real capital cities of the world. For, in London, are to be found close together the institutions which reflect the origin of the values which the Americans hold dear: the Palace of Westminster, the home of parliamentary liberty; Westminster Abbey, a spiritual jewel at the heart of the nation, a place not only of the coronation, but also of the burial, of Kings and Queens; Buckingham Palace, where the daily ceremony of the Changing of the Guard reminds us of the solemnity and majesty of the monarch; and the Royal Courts of Justice, where the Judges sit, in scarlet and black, giving reasoned judgments. These shows make a rich feast for people from other countries within the English-speaking nation who perhaps lack colour and ceremony at home. Most tourists do not bother to enquire what lies behind the trappings of state: but at least they experience awe and wonder at the brilliance of government. Some may be led to consider that these shows are reflections of the great powers of mind and government which exist in everybody.

When they go to Stratford-upon-Avon, Americans pay homage to the master-poet, William Shakespeare, who helped shape their traditions for them through the plays that he wrote about the English nation.

The Queen is also said to be the 'Fountain of Honour'. Just as the Queen's personal life and conduct must be above reproach, so she should honour and give titles only to those men and women who will set the best examples. The honours that the Queen can award, such as dukedoms, earldoms, baronies, knighthoods, originally carried certain duties with them: an earl, for example, was the man in charge of a county of the kingdom, and a knight was someone who did military service for the King or Queen. Nowadays these honours tend to be granted, on the advice of the Prime Minister, to men and women who have already done good service for the nation. And there have been occasions, recently, when Prime Ministers allowed their personal likes and dislikes to dictate whom they should recommend for honours from the Queen: which is a pity, because the honours system serves a useful purpose, as a reward for dedicated work in arts, sciences, literature, politics and the many other fields of human endeavour.

One of the highest offices is to become Her Majesty's Privy Councillor, that is, someone who shares the confidence of the Queen concerning the most important (and perhaps very secret) matters of state. Privy Councillors are allowed to put 'Right Honourable' before their names. The Prime Minister of the day and his cabinet colleagues become Privy Councillors when they take office; but whereas a man or woman can only become Prime Minister or Minister for a limited period of time, while they retain the support of Parliament, a Privy Councillor is appointed for life. He or she is required to swear an oath, the words of which indicate the seriousness of the duty the Privy Councillor undertakes to perform. Blackstone says, about this duty, that it has seven aspects:

> 1. To advise the king according to the best of his cunning and discretion. 2. To advise for the king's honour and good of the public, without partiality through affection, love, need, doubt or dread. 3. To keep the king's council secret. 4. To avoid corruption. 5. To help and strengthen the execution of what shall be there resolved. 6. To withstand all persons who would attempt the contrary. And, lastly, in general, 7. To observe, keep, and do all that a good and true counsellor ought to do to his sovereign lord.

One of the meanings of the word 'cabinet' is a small room where people can meet privately to discuss affairs. In the old days a King would meet some of his most trusted Privy Councillors in a cabinet room. Among them would be the Secretaries of State—that is, men who were charged with the great secrets of the state. This is very necessary because it would not do for everyone to know about these secrets, otherwise they might become frightened, or use them for their own benefit at the expense of others. Now this word 'cabinet' has come to mean the Prime Minister and the other Ministers appointed by the Queen from among the Members of Parliament belonging to the party with the largest number of votes at the last election.

Today the Privy Council has over three hundred members. It never meets as a body; and the Queen looks to the cabinet for her advice and for the day to day running of the affairs of the country. But if ever there was a serious crisis in government, then the Queen might call on the Privy Councillors to assist her in coming to the right decision for the good of the nation. She would then have the wisdom and the experience to draw on of men and women from all political parties, yet bound together by the common oath and duty described by Blackstone.

It has to be understood that, in the end, the Queen is responsible, under God, for the good government of the nation. No-one else can do that work for her. She has a great and lonely task. How great and how lonely can be shown by the courageous decision of her representative in Australia, the Governor-General, Sir John Kerr, when he acted a few years ago to dismiss a Prime Minister and a cabinet which were becoming tyrannical—that is, they thought themselves above the law. You will remember that the basic principle of our Constitution (as well as the Australian, for they derive their liberties from us) is that the King must be under no man, but under God and the law, for the law makes the King. Thus, the Australian Prime Minister and his colleagues were behaving as though the law were meant to serve only their purposes. It appeared that the good order of the state was breaking down.

The Governor-General, on the advice of the Chief Justice of Australia, acted swiftly and, as he said, in accordance with his oath of office, his responsibilities, authority and duty. Twice since then the people of Australia have refused to vote that Prime Minister back into power. Yet the Governor-General himself was treated very badly. Many people said that he should not have done what he did; they spurned and humiliated him, and finally he left office. Sir John Kerr is a fine example of an honourable man who put the interests of the people above himself and his own safety.

It is very much to be hoped that Her Majesty, or a future King or Queen, is not put into that position. Our present Queen is much loved and admired. She would only exercise the 'supreme executive power' by herself in the gravest emergency; and then she would rely, as she said when she was Princess Elizabeth, on the strength and support of the whole people.

We sing our anthem, 'God Save The Queen'. It is a prayer as well as an anthem. We ask God to save the Queen because in her lie the peace, prosperity and good order of us all.

6
Parliament

. . . Parliament is a *deliberative* assembly of *one* nation, with *one* interest, that of the whole — where not local purposes, not local prejudices, ought to guide, but the general good, resulting from the general reason of the whole.—*Edmund Burke*

This word 'Parliament' also needs to be looked up in a good dictionary. Originally it meant just people talking together, and you could have all kinds of 'parliaments', including, for example, monks gossiping together in the cloisters after dinner: a practice which was frowned on by the abbot. It was not until the thirteenth century that the word came to mean the deliberative assembly which Edmund Burke talks about, where the great issues and problems of the nation are debated.

That is another curious word, 'debate'. If you look it up, the dictionary will tell you that it is formed from two Latin words meaning 'to beat down'. It conjures up a picture of men in armour clouting each other, and trying to knock each other to the ground; rather than the image we have of a debate in the House of Commons, where Members of Parliament do not attack each other physically (or hardly ever), and the proceedings are conducted by speeches. But—do you remember we mentioned the mace of the House of Commons, which is carried by the Serjeant-at-Arms before the Speaker when he enters the House, and which is placed on brackets on the Table while the Speaker is in the Chair? The mace was, of course, a battle club. And, in some of the earliest stories known to mankind, the power to reason is described as a club—a club to hit false ideas on the head.

So the idea of beating down, or fighting, is not inaccurate. We have to understand that fighting can take place on several levels: when we see films of soldiers fighting in wars, this is just the result of another struggle which has already taken place in the world of mind, between conflicting ideas, opinions and feelings. Usually, before the battle lines have been drawn on the ground, the rulers of states which are quarrelling have said, in words, why it is they propose going to war. They will always say they are going to fight for what they think is right: no-one ever says they are going to fight for what they think is wrong. In such situations, where there is a dispute, the use of reason is so important: for it acts like a light in the mind, clearly showing what is rightfully to be done.

There is a story about ancient India, at a time when violence and doubt and fear were all about, and men lacked law. A very holy teacher went around the country debating with the men of ideas and the men in authority. Everywhere he won these debates because his use of reason was so powerful that he clearly showed, through his words, that his opponents' ideas were wrong. According to the rules of debate, his opponents immediately gave up their wrong ideas and followed him. Thus he began to unify the nation and prevent strife.

Now, that story is very interesting because the principle of debating is still the same. First of all, there has to be a 'Motion': there is no good having a debate about the first thing that comes into your head. A Motion is a form of words on a question of the day about which men can feel strongly. Thus it must be a topic which *moves* them to speak. The first speaker is the mover of the motion, because he seeks to persuade others to follow him. The opposer speaks next, against the motion, and, equally, he seeks the support of the others. Usually, all speakers in a debate are allowed to speak only once to the question: otherwise the debate becomes an argument, which is not the same thing. Then, when everyone who wants to has spoken, the motion is put to the vote. As we saw, the original meaning of 'vote' was 'vow'—you give your vow, or promise, to give up your own ideas and follow the man who has convinced you through his speech.

Not always can it be said—particularly today—that the speaker who is most reasonable is the one who is going to win. Words always have their effect. They can play on the emotions or feelings of people; and the voice of a skilled speaker, who knows precisely what he is doing, and has a wicked purpose, can lead them into mischief. In Germany, fifty years ago, they had a leader called Hitler who was intensely evil: yet he had a command over words which enchanted and enthralled the Germans. He always claimed that he wanted only to serve the best interests of the German nation and that these could only be achieved through warfare and destruction. Under the spell of his voice, the Germans went to war and got what he promised them—destruction, but for themselves.

This is not to say that reason only sometimes works. It always works. The reasonable is the good and true. It is the law. In the words of an Upanishad:

> Law is truth. Who speaks the truth, speaks the law; who speaks the law, speaks the truth; they are the same.

And, in this country in particular, there is a strong tradition to follow the reasonable man. The English favour reason because they know that unreasonable behaviour always leads to misery. 'Reason is the life of the law,' said Judge Coke—the judge who stood up against the unreasonable proposals of the King, James I, in the seventeenth century. And, a century later, the great parliamentarian, Edmund Burke, wrote a book called *Reflections on the Revolution in France*, which shone the great light of reason on all the terrible, destructive things which were being done there in the name of liberty, equality and fraternity. In fact, he clearly demonstrated that the constitution of France—that by which the French nation stood together— was being torn apart. At the time there was real danger of revolution and civil war spreading to this country. Edmund Burke's work largely checked this evil impulse. His book, which was read by many people and translated into other languages, was concerned with the many fine principles and institutions at work in this country: he said that they could be reformed or reshaped to meet the needs of the day, provided one knew what one was doing; but they ought never to be destroyed for the sake of the ideas of a few men, who thoughtlessly undid the work and wisdom of centuries.

Let us now take an imaginary journey into the Palace of

Westminster, to visit the two great Chambers where debates are held: that of the House of Commons and that of the House of Lords. It is called the Palace of Westminster because, historically, this was once a palace of the kings. The building that we see today, however, dates back only to the last century, after a fire destroyed the old palace, when someone carelessly burned 'tally sticks', the pieces of wood in which they used to cut notches representing money received from taxpayers by the government.

Everyone knows the Palace of Westminster, or the Houses of Parliament as it is sometimes called, by the famous clock in its tall tower called 'Big Ben'. The clock was probably named after Sir Benjamin Hall, the First Commissioner for Works at the time when it was installed. For such a huge clock, it is remarkably accurate; and has only stopped through accidents like a Member of Parliament prodding its machinery with his umbrella or a broom being left on a shaft. Above the clock is a light, called the 'Ayrton Light' after another Commissioner for Works, which always shines when the House of Commons is sitting after nightfall. You can stand in Parliament Square and see it, in a little house high up, above the clockface. During the last war it was extinguished, of course, as it would have been a guide for enemy aeroplanes; but when it was re-lit in 1945 the Speaker of the House of Commons said this:

> I pray that, with God's blessing, this light will shine henceforth not only as an outward and visible sign that the Parliament of a free people is assembled in free debate but also that it may shine as a beacon of sure hope in a sadly torn and distracted world.

In the clock-tower itself is a prison where people can be confined by order of the House of Commons, including its own Members if they happen to be unruly. This is a reminder both that there is a common law especially for Parliament, so that its dignity and authority are not abused; and that in many respects Parliament originated as a court of law ('The High Court of Parliament') by which the great grievances of the people might be brought before the king.

We go into the Palace by way of St Stephen's Porch. On our left is the most historic part of the Palace, Westminster Hall, originally built by a king, William Rufus, in 1099. This great hall, with a beautiful oak beam roof constructed in the reign of Richard II, has survived the fires and the bombings. It has been the scene, over the centuries, of many magnificent state occasions, such as coronation feasts and, in recent times, the lyings-in-state of dead kings. It has also been the scene of great trials: most notably that of a king himself, King Charles I, when he was ordered to be executed by Oliver Cromwell and his friends, in 1649, following the last civil war to ravage this nation. You remember that we said a nation cannot have two sovereigns: and the dispute in the seventeenth century was over exactly this, whether the King-in-Parliament (meaning the King acting with the advice and consent of the Lords and Commons), or the King alone, was sovereign. Poor Charles acted foolishly, and tried to rule alone, when both he and his father, James I, had been clearly advised that the King must be under no man, but under God and under the law made by the King in consultation with Parliament.

But going back even further, Westminster Hall was where the law courts met. Nowadays they are further down the river, in the Strand, at the Royal Courts of Justice. It must have been a busy and noisy scene when several courts met at the same time, in different parts of Westminster Hall. Then you would have seen the judges in their robes sitting on high, and around them clusters of excited people, arguing and disputing.

Once through St Stephen's Porch we are in St Stephen's Hall, a very famous part of the Palace indeed; for this is the site of a chapel, St Stephen's Chapel, where the House of Commons met from 1547 to 1834. It is interesting that the Commons debated for all those years in a place of worship: the Speaker sat in his high chair in front of the altar. Members still bow towards the Speaker's chair on entering or leaving their present Chamber—a reminder of the time when they did so in reverence to the altar.

St Stephen's Chapel was where so many famous debates took place, so many battles in words for the freedoms which we cherish as a nation. When you come across a word with 'dom' in it, you are looking at one of our oldest English words— 'doom', which meant 'law' but also meant 'place'. 'Freedom', the place to be free; also the law of the free, which signifies duties. The two are the same, law and place: because, under the law, performing one's duties one is in the place of the free.

Statues of famous statesmen of the past line St Stephen's. Here you may find the statue of Edmund Burke, whose words we rely on so much in this book. And, in the floor of St Stephen's, you can see brass studs marking the former position of the Speaker's Chair and the Table of the House—where Charles I came when he burst into the House of Commons with armed men to arrest five of its members. That was the last time a king tried to invade the freedom of the House—the place to be free—and imprison its Members. Angrily the King looked round the Chamber, but none of the five men he wanted could be seen. He tried to bully the Speaker: 'Are any of these persons in the House? Do you see any of them? Where are they?'

Speaker Lenthall knelt before his King. Humbly but firmly he made his reply: 'May it please your Majesty, I have neither eyes to see nor tongue to speak in this place, but as the House is pleased to direct me, whose servant I am here.' He was telling the King that it was not right for him to try to take the law into his own hands and arrest men who had been debating the affairs of the nation, responsibly.

So it has not always been an easy task, being Speaker of the House of Commons. The title meant, historically, that he spoke for the House of Commons to the King and the Lords. He told the King what the Commons wanted. If the monarch did not like it and got angry, as Charles did, the Speaker himself might suffer. Therefore Members of Parliament were reluctant to assume the position and, once elected, a new Speaker had to be dragged to the Chair of the House. Even today when there is no fear of arrest or punishment by the Queen—no King or Queen has attempted to enter the House of Commons since the time of Charles I—the custom is maintained of taking a new Speaker by the arms and literally forcing him to sit in the Speaker's Chair.

At the beginning of each Parliament, the Speaker goes to the House of Lords to represent the Commons there. On his return to the House of Commons he tells Members this:

> I have, in your name, and on your behalf, laid claim, by humble petition to Her Majesty, to all your ancient and undoubted rights and privileges, particularly freedom of speech in debate, freedom from arrest, freedom of access to Her Majesty whenever occasion may require, and that the most favourable construction may be placed on all your proceedings . . . All these Her Majesty has been pleased to allow and confirm, in as ample a manner as they have ever been granted or confirmed by herself or any of her Royal predecessors.

Notice that none of these rights are taken for granted: they have to be asked for from the monarch. That is just recognition by the House of Commons that they meet in peace, undisturbed by threats against them, only because the Queen herself is strong enough and powerful enough to protect them. If they abused this protection long enough, making bitter attacks on each other, in words, or against the institutions of the nation, then one would expect the ability of the Queen to protect them in peace to weaken also. It is called 'The Queen's Peace'. All parts of our government have to work together to preserve this; and it is an example of the unity of will and action in the mind of the nation. From time to time, in our history, the King's Peace has been very narrow, extending perhaps to the person of the King himself, the place where he was living and holding court and to the highways along which he travelled. But now it extends to the whole nation, because we recognise it and want it for ourselves and are prepared to work for it.

If we go further forward into the Palace of Westminster, we may catch sight of the Speaker's Procession making its stately way towards the Commons' Chamber. Before the Speaker is the Serjeant-at-arms, carrying the mace; then Mr Speaker in his black and gold gown and wearing a long wig; and then the Speaker's Chaplain, who will say prayers before the sitting of the House. As they go through the corridors, policemen call 'Mr Speaker' and everyone has to stand still and Members of Parliament bow as the procession passes.

Let us go up into the public gallery of the House of Commons. We shall not be allowed in until the Members have said prayers. But, once inside, we are looking down into the most famous debating chamber in the world. It is a place of green and gold and light-coloured wood, and there is soft, warm lighting coming from panels in the long ceiling; so it is rather like coming into a perpetual summer afternoon.

The Chamber of the Commons is not big. It is arranged in the same way as the choir of a church, with long, green leather benches on either side, and the great, carved Speaker's Chair and the long Table of the House between the benches at the other end. We can see the silver mace now resting on brackets on the Table and the Speaker in his long wig sitting back in his chair, almost like a figure exhibited in a showcase. Before him, sitting at the end of the Table, are two Clerk-Assistants of the House, wearing short wigs, busy writing. The Table is strewn with papers and with books.

Members of Parliament sit on the benches on either side of the Speaker. Those who sit on the right of the Speaker belong to the political party which currently has the most popular support in the country: on the front bench sit members of the Cabinet and other Ministers of the Crown. On the benches to the left of the Speaker sit Members who belong to other political parties: they are called 'Her Majesty's Loyal Opposition'. They often oppose what is suggested by the Queen's Ministers of the day; but they are loyal, too, because they might be called on in turn to 'form a government': that is, to provide Members who will become Her Majesty's Ministers and, in consultation with the Queen, run the day-by-day affairs of the country. If you look down at the carpet which separates the two sides of the House you will see a broad red stripe running down each side. No Member of the House can cross the red stripe while he is speaking from his side of the Chamber. This is one of the rules to prevent clashes between members if and when tempers begin to rise.

The stillness and reason and, on occasions, the sense of humour of the Speaker are most important in preserving order in a debate. As we have said, the House of Commons is the emotional centre of our government: here is where the opinions and beliefs at large in the mind of the community are given utterance in words. Ideas which are at work in the life of everyone at a particular period of time require emotional support: that is, the love and willingness of people must respond to the ideas if they are to govern our actions. When ideas change, or are in question, this means that love and willingness are being given in other directions: and the Commons and the Ministers must take account of these changes. They are usually very sensitive to the changes in men's desires but, if they have been giving their support to ideas which they strongly believe in as offering the best course for the nation, then naturally there will sometimes be bitterness and anger in the House when these ideas are challenged. In the analogy of the chariot, in the Upanishad, it was said that the horses were senses, objects of desire the roads. We as a people might want certain things for a period of time and then desire other things: it is like the chariot being taken by the horses down one road, coming to a crossroads and then a decision having to be made which road to follow. The horses might want to go one way: and sometimes they will have to be checked and steered by the reins if that way will lead them to disaster. The horses might not like it, but ultimately they have to obey the reins.

So, in the House of Commons, the Speaker has to intervene from time to time to keep order. He has very great powers to guide debate. He needs them when tempers begin to rise. But a good Speaker relies more on appeals to good sense and to reason, and he will use humour to dissolve anger. The present Speaker, Mr George Thomas, is a fine and deeply religious man. He is also a Welshman, which means he speaks English with a delightful, musical lilt. Once tempers were beginning to show themselves in the House, and a Member got up to complain that he had not understood a word of what another member had said. Mr Thomas rose to his feet, which is always a stilling effect, seeing that majestic figure in black and gold with its long wig towering over the House, and said this: 'Members of his House come from all parts of the country, and they have many different accents, many different ways of speaking. I only wish I had an accent myself.' The House broke into laughter. Tension went because, of course, Mr Speaker has this soft, Welsh sing-song in his voice.

Another rule is that when Members speak they always turn slightly to address their remarks to the chair in which Mr Speaker is sitting quietly. Thus they are not addressing each other personally, but through the Chair of the House. This, too, has a stilling and ordering effect on debate.

The Chamber is, in fact, not large enough to seat all the 630 or so Members. If they all turned up at once, they would have to sit in the aisles or stand round the Speaker's Chair. This is because the House of Commons is designed to encourage quiet, reasonable debate, where Members can speak without raising their voices or lecturing each other.

7

The House of Commons

Party is a body of men united for promoting by their joint
endeavours the national interest upon some particular principle
in which they are all agreed.—*Edmund Burke*

In our imaginary journey into the Palace of Westminster we
found ourselves, in the last chapter, looking down from the
public gallery on the House of Commons in session.

We have arrived at the start of the parliamentary day, shortly
after 2.30 in the afternoon. You might think that was a late start
to a day; but we have been concerned, in this country, that
Members of Parliament should not cut themselves off from the
work in the community that each of them has been trained to
do, such as lawyers, businessmen, accountants and so on. This
has two effects: Members of Parliament can return to their jobs
full-time if they are not re-elected; and they are not led to feel
that being an MP is a separate vocation, somehow superior to
everyone else's. It is important that Members of Parliament
maintain their links with the community, for they are the reins
in the analogy of the chariot—and the function of reins is to tell
the driver what the horses are feeling and doing.

Most Members of Parliament, therefore, spend part of the
day on their own affairs and come to Parliament in the
afternoons, staying sometimes until late at night, to discuss
and debate on committees and in the Chamber of the House.
They are paid for being MP's, but certainly not lavishly; and it
is not always easy for them to combine their private lives,
earning more money to help support themselves and their
families, with their public duties to the government of the
country. In the old days Parliament met for brief periods in the
year, which meant that Members could spend more time on
personal business. Nowadays, when Parliament is in session
most of the year, and the House sits frequently until the early

58   *The Young People's Book of the Constitution*

hours of the morning, there are tired Members emerging from the Commons Chamber to hear the policemen cry 'Who goes home?' through the darkened corridors.

The Prime Minister and the other Ministers of the Crown, of course, have to devote themselves entirely to the affairs of the nation. They are on call all the time, just as the Queen is, to deal with any emergencies which might arise. Their service must be utterly dedicated, while they hold office under the Crown—yet they are still Members of Parliament, and are paid extra money as Ministers so that they will not have to earn a living outside.

If you look along the benches, to the right of Mr Speaker, you will see the Ministers sitting together on the front bench. They do not look any different from the other Members sitting elsewhere in the House. They are first and foremost Members of this House; and only when they have the support and approval of their fellow-Members are they allowed to continue as Ministers of the Crown. They have to present their ideas to the House; they have to debate them with other Members; they have to explain what they have been doing in the interests of the nation.

A Minister is on his feet at this moment, answering a question put to him by an ordinary Member of Parliament. This is Question Time, which lasts for about an hour, at the start of the day's business. The purpose of asking questions is to get from Ministers information about what is happening in government, so that the House knows what is going on; and also to press Ministers to take some action, if there is a need for something to be done. You will remember that the Queen and her Ministers are responsible for the active part of government; that is, the part which actually gives orders for things to be done and sees that they are carried out. The two Houses of Parliament, the House of Lords and the House of Commons, are the deliberative assembly, in the words of Edmund Burke which appear above Chapter 6 of this book. They deliberate, they discuss, they talk about the measures which the active part of government wish to take for the benefit of the nation. From these discussions the light of reason should arise to show the path forward. If what is proposed is shown to be reasonable, and in the best interests of the people, then the Lords and Commons will give their 'consent'. That word 'consent' means 'to feel together'. Thus, in the view of Parliament, the mind and the heart of the people will come together to make it possible for what is suggested to take place. In the Upanishad it said: 'Senses are the horses, objects of desire the roads. When Self is joined to body, mind, sense, none but He enjoys.' It is important to join all these up, and when the senses of a nation are connected with its mind, through the reins of Parliament, then it happens that the right road can be taken.

So, it is necessary for Members of Parliament not only to be informed about what is going on in the country at large but also about what Ministers are doing, or proposing to do. Ministers of the Crown are given power to act in the name of the Queen. It is most important that they keep within the power they are given and do not try to act outside, or above, the law which grants them power. Therefore Ministers are required to answer questions which are put to them about how they have been conducting affairs.

A Member of Parliament might ask: 'Will the Right Honourable gentleman tell the House what is the current strength of the police force in London?' He calls the Minister 'Right Honourable' because he is usually a Privy Councillor.

The Minister's reply will be brief and to the point. In answer to a question seeking information like this he will probably just state the number of policemen.

Then the Member of Parliament can ask a supplementary question which is often more to the real point he is trying to make. He might say: 'In view of that answer, and of the fact that crime is increasing in the capital, what plans does the Right Honourable gentleman have to enlarge the police force?' The Minister will have had two or three days' notice of the first question; but none at all of the supplementary question. He will have to answer immediately. Sometimes on how he answers the question from an ordinary Member will depend the confidence and trust of the House of Commons in himself and all the other Ministers in the Cabinet. If the House is not satisfied with the reply he gives, Members may ask afterwards for time to debate the whole matter in detail.

It is no wonder, then, that Ministers have said how nervous they are before Question Time in the House. Still, it keeps them in place; and reminds them that they have to account for themselves to their fellow-Members.

Following Question Time, we may see the House debate a Public Bill. A Bill is an Act of Parliament before it has passed through all the stages of discussion and voting in the House of Commons and the House of Lords and has been given the force of law by the Queen's assent. The words of the Bill will be discussed, amended or deleted during the process of debate. If either the House of Commons or the Lords do not like what the Bill says, as a whole, they can vote against it and it will not become law on that occasion; or the Queen could refuse her assent, something which she would only do if the Bill required her to do grievous wrong. 'The Queen can do no wrong.' She can only do right.

The process of making an Act of Parliament is called 'legislating': that comes from two Latin words meaning 'bringing a law' to the people. The law already is: it is the Will of God in creation. We have seen how the law runs through the whole of government, giving unity to the various parts; acting through the Queen in Parliament to direct the nation. That law may be made clear by the Judges sitting in their courts, or it may be necessary, for a time, for Parliament to make a statute (which is another word for an Act of Parliament). 'Statute' comes from a Latin word, to do with standing. Thus, Parliament may give standing, or status, to a certain idea, person or thing for a time in order for the law to act through it. There are lots of old statutes in the books of law which are now forgotten and not put into practice: that is because their time has gone and they are of no further use. So Parliament makes temporary law, to deal with the effects of great problems and troubles which afflict the people. In that sense Parliament is rather like a doctor who attends you when you are ill: in fact, some Judges of many centuries ago said a statute was the 'remedy the Parliament hath resolved and appointed to cure the disease of the commonwealth'. When the body of the nation is sound, we do not have to have doctors and sometimes painful remedies: we rely on the Common Law, the unchanging law, which is discoverable by the light of reason, and put into words for us by the Judges to govern our everyday behaviour.

Bills were originally petitions, or prayers, from the common people of the country, asking the King to make a statute to right some great wrong or grievance that they had. The King, for his part, needed money to maintain the government of the nation. That money had to be supplied by the people. The King would summon a Parliament to ask for money, as well as advice on the problems of the day. Parliament would then present the petitions, or bills, to the King with a request that the grievances be dealt with before they taxed the people. It is still a principle that only the House of Commons can raise a tax on the people: that is, order everyone to pay money to cover the expenses of government. The word 'taxation' is related to the Latin word *tangere*, meaning 'to touch'. When the first parliaments were established, six hundred years ago, the knights and the gentlemen who represented the counties and the towns were summoned by the King in these words: *Quod omnes tangit, ab omnibus approbetur*—'What touches all should be approved by all'. As taxation spread, as more and more people were 'touched' or affected by the needs of government to raise money, so voting for Members of Parliament expanded until today practically everyone over the age of eighteen both has the right to vote and the duty to pay taxation. Thus are rights and duties connected. If you pay taxes in one form or another, you should also have the right to say whom you think is the best person to represent you in the House of Commons, and see that the money is wisely spent. On the other hand, when people believe that they are being asked to pay too much by way of taxation, they can become bitter about their right to vote and say that it does not mean much: or they try to avoid their duty to pay taxes. This is a dangerous state of affairs, and

Members of Parliament are wise to keep in mind that the people they represent will become angry if the burden of taxation becomes too great.

An old Chinese sage had some wise things to say about this subject: 'The people starve because those in authority over them devour too many taxes; that is why they starve.The people are difficult to govern because those placed over them are meddlesome; that is why they are difficult to govern.'

But, even though only the House of Commons may approve a tax on the people, an ordinary Member of Parliament could not get up in the House and ask for money to be spent in one way or another. This is because only the Queen and her Prime Minister and his cabinet know how much money is required and for what purpose. Erskine May, the great parliamentary authority, describes it thus:

> The Crown demands money, the Commons grant it, and the Lords assent to the grant; but the Commons do not vote money unless it be required by the Crown; nor impose or augment taxes, unless such taxation be necessary for the public service as declared by the Crown through its constitutional advisers.

So we may look down from the public gallery and observe a debate on a Bill. A Bill has to pass through three 'readings' before it can be sent up to the House of Lords for their consideration; when it has also received three readings in the House of Lords it is ready for the Royal Assent by the Queen, and then becomes an Act of Parliament, that is, Parliament has acted to 'cure the disease of the commonwealth', in the words of those old Judges. The Bill becomes an Act, becomes lawful, when the Royal Commissioners on behalf of the Queen say the following words in old, Norman French: *La Reine le veult* ('The Queen wishes it').

The three readings date back to the time before printing, when Bills had to be read out loud. Nowadays, of course, Bills are printed so that each Member has a copy. The first reading is when the Bill is introduced to the House, and is a formality, going through 'on the nod', as they say. The second stage, or reading, is much more exciting: this is when a Member, usually a Minister, has to make a speech describing why the Bill is necessary, in the view of the Cabinet, and proposing the question 'That the Bill be now read a second time'. When he has finished, a senior Member from the Opposition side will make a speech saying why his party opposes the Bill, and usually end with an amendment 'That the Bill be read this day six months.' All this means is that, if the Opposition succeeded in convincing the House that the principle of the Bill is wrong, the Bill fails. It will not be read again in six months' time, or at all.

After the main speakers, Members on both sides of the House try to 'catch the Speaker's eye' to be allowed to rise in their places and address the House on the merits of the Bill. The Speaker tries to be fair about this: he chooses Members in turn from both sides of the House. Once having spoken, a Member is not allowed to say anything again, except perhaps to clarify what he has said, or to raise a point of order in connection with the rules of debate.

However, the main speaker for the government side is allowed, at the end of the debate, when the Speaker senses that everything that needs to be said has been said, to draw all the threads together in a final speech. No doubt he pleads with the House to vote for the motion. And he knows that the Bill is likely to pass, because on a vote the Government has the support of the majority of the Members in the House. There is, nevertheless, a feeling of drama about a vote, especially when the governing side has not many more Members than the Opposition, and some may be ill or out of the country.

The Speaker rises from his chair. He says to the House: 'The question is, that the word "now" do stand part of the question.' You remember that the original question that the House had before it to decide was 'That the bill be now read a second time'. The Opposition have sought to change it by amending the word 'now' to 'this day six months'. So the House will have to decide whether it wants the Bill to be read a second time, in which case it will answer 'Yes' to the question.

'As many as are of that opinion,' the Speaker says, 'say

"Aye".' The government benches roar 'Aye'.

The Speaker then says: 'As many as are of the contrary opinion say "No".' 'No', shout the Opposition benches.

'I think the Ayes have it', Mr Speaker states. If the Opposition parties do not accept the outcome of the vote they then cry 'No!' vigorously. This means that an actual count of Members voting either way must be taken. 'Clear the lobby,' orders the Speaker and sits down again.

Bells start ringing throughout the Palace of Westminster, summoning all Members to the vote. Tellers from both sides of the House, two Members from the right of the Speaker and two from his left, take up their positions in the division lobbies. These are long corridors stretching the whole length of the Commons Chamber with doors at each end. The 'Ayes' lobby is to the right of the Speaker, and the 'Noes' lobby to the left. Members go into the lobby in which they wish to vote.

When they are nearly all in—and they may have to hurry from all parts of the huge building—the Speaker rises in the empty Chamber and says: 'Lock the doors.' One set of doors is then locked; the other set is then opened and Members start to come back into the House, bowing to the tellers who are counting them.

A member is required to go into the lobby which accords with what he shouted in the House. It is a rule that what he actually said in the House, either 'Aye' or 'No', binds him; and he cannot, after that, cast his vote in the other lobby. The House recognises in this that what a man says is of the greatest importance, and he must keep to his word. Also, he will not be much liked if he goes into the lobby of the opposing parties: if the Bill is considered to be of major concern to the country, the party to which the Member belongs will already have decided whether to vote for it or against it. The parties have Members called 'party whips'. That name pretty well tells you what these Members have to do: they have to see that Members belonging to that party attend the House and that they vote in the right lobbies. Each member will have received a letter from the party whip telling him or her how to vote on a particular Bill: if the title of the Bill is underlined three times in the letter this is called a 'three-line whip', and the Member will be in serious trouble with his own party if, short of illness, he fails to attend and vote accordingly.

When the House has re-assembled after a division, the tellers advance to the table, bowing to the Speaker, and handing up a piece of paper with the result written on it. The Speaker announces the result, which may be something like the following: 'The Ayes to the right, 320, the Noes to the left, 306.'

This means that the Bill has been read a second time. It can now go forward to what is called the 'committee stage', in which a committee of Members of Parliament examine it line by line to see that the words are right to express the principle which the House has now adopted by giving the Bill a second reading. In committee, Members are not allowed to debate the merits of the Bill as a whole but only the words and phrases of it. They seek now to have the intention of Parliament put in the clearest possible way.

When the Bill comes back to the House, perhaps weeks later, it is said to be 'reported to the House' in the improved form in which it left the Committee. Now Members may attack it again; but if they do not succeed it is given its third reading and is ready to go forward to the House of Lords for another three readings.

Before leaving the Chamber of the House of Commons, let us consider the question of parties. We have seen how the very Chamber itself divides into left and right of the Speaker: and that the party sitting on the benches to the right form the government of the day, while the party or parties sitting on the left are 'Her Majesty's Loyal Opposition'. This division of the House broadly corresponds with the beliefs and feelings of the people. There is always a will in the people to keep to what they know and love best, their traditions and their characteristics; there is also, from time to time, a desire to change things, to reform and to adapt. All governments, throughout the world, reflect these two basic desires: one a desire to stand still for a time, to reflect, and to save energy; the other, to move forward and shape new ways of living and working. The first can be called a conservative instinct; and the second can be called progressive.

The political parties express these views. There is a Conservative party which seeks to govern in accordance with well-tried methods; and there are progressive parties, 'Labour' and 'Liberal', which are concerned with change and reform. Both elements are essential and natural: individuals are like this, too; after an exciting time, when new things are always happening, you probably feel like having a rest and settling down to see how the new things work.

This process is called 'the pendulum of politics'. Like the pendulum of a clock, opinion sways backwards and forwards between conservatism and reform. At elections people are asked to decide which party they want to govern for the next five years, and the answer will come: the party of change or the party of no change. Generally speaking, for long periods, people are content with little or no change; but sometimes new ideas come along and appeal to people's desires and willingness to try something different.

The major ideas which govern a nation usually shift about once in thirty or forty years, which is about the time they take to grow and flower from the seeds planted in the universities. A young man or woman goes to university in his or her early twenties and studies and picks up ideas which are usually different from the ideas ruling at the time: newspapers are always telling their readers about discontent amongst university students. But that is natural, too. And then, in thirty or forty years, those same young men and women have grown considerably older, perhaps wiser: but, in any event, they will have the task of helping to govern the nation. Then they are likely to try to put into effect the ideas which they picked up in their studies.

These ideas usually take one of two forms: either they are related to the individual, what he can do for himself with the minimum of interference from the rulers; or they are related to what can be done by people acting together in a group. Since the end of the Second World War about forty years ago, this country—and, indeed, a large part of the world—has been governed by the idea that the State should be active in providing work and services for its people. There have been great schemes, like the National Health Service, with hospitals and doctors and dentists paid for out of taxation, so that poor people do not have to worry about paying the bills if they fall sick; and large industries run by the government so that men are not out of work. The trouble has been that they have cost a lot of money and people have had to pay high taxes: this has made them poorer still, and so the government has had to provide more services. So it has gone round in circles. When this happens, the money required to pay for it all has lessened in value; more money has been needed to pay for the same things. Recently people have got tired of all this and wanted to do more things for themselves, as individuals, without the government interfering too much and directing them. So the idea has changed—away from the State and more towards the individual.

The Labour Party, since the war, has been in power as the governing party several times: and each time it has been elected it has brought in a whole programme of Acts of Parliament designed to regulate people's lives in detail. They have been acting under a principle stated by a writer called Jeremy Bentham, nearly two hundred years ago. He said: 'The greatest happiness of the greatest number is the foundation of morals and legislation.' That sounds all right: but it does mean that some people, who are not in the greatest number, will be less happy and perhaps miserable; and it also means that someone else, someone in government, can tell us what happiness means. Up to a point, that is fine; but the natural love of freedom, which is an Englishman's birthright, then begins to show itself, and people begin to say, 'Well, I think I know how to be happy without being told all the time by the government. I wish they wouldn't interfere so much. I can do things quite well by myself, thank you.'

The Conservative Party has also been in power several times since the war. This party represents the stable, traditional element in our nation. But it, too, has had to carry out programmes of public works and services under the rule of prevailing ideas. They have not gone about it as far and as fast as the Labour Party because, of course, their nature makes them cautious to change too much. They do not pass as many Acts of Parliament when they are in power, preferring to let individuals alone and encouraging them to become wealthy by their own efforts.

The Liberals, another main party, are not very large in number in Parliament. Historically, they were the party of reform; but that role they had to give up to the Labour Party when it became popular among the masses early this century. Liberals believe very much in individual freedom. You might say that Liberals, today, occupy the middle ground between the extremes of the Conservative and Labour Parties.

If you ever get the chance, you might go and see one of Gilbert and Sullivan's comic operas, *Iolanthe*. In that you will hear the Lord Chancellor sing:

> I often think it's comical
> How Nature always does contrive
> That every boy and every gal,
> That's born into the world alive,
> Is either a little Liberal,
> Or else a little Conservative.

There is a lot of truth in that little song. Our political parties just reflect the fact that some of us always want a quiet life, not being bothered; and others of us are always trying to get things changed!

8

The House of Lords

Nobility is the symbol of mind.—*Walter Bagehot*

When the Queen opens Parliament and sits on the throne in the splendid, glittering House of Lords, we are seeing Parliament as it once was, when the monarch was present at all its sessions. Now, except for the great ceremonial occasions, the throne at the end of the House of Lords remains empty, although Privy Councillors and the eldest sons of lords may sit on the steps to the throne during debates.

But, in the opening of a new session of parliament, Queen, Lords and Commons meet together briefly, to hear the Speech from the Throne, which is written for the Queen by her Prime Minister, giving the policy which her Cabinet Ministers hope to put into effect. It is a pity, in a way, that Ministers feel it necessary to tell us all they intend to do over the next few years; because they cannot possibly know at the time what events they will have to meet—and yet they feel bound to try to do it all, even when it appears it will not work, simply because it was all there in the opening speech. They feel they may have failed, and will not be re-elected by the people, if they do not achieve most of what they set out to do. This is the reason why so many modern Parliaments are burdened with having to consider long lists of Bills, setting out the steps by which these ideas can be put into practice; rather than having the time and freedom to discuss the affairs of the country as they actually happen.

This method of addressing the Lords and Commons by the reigning King or Queen goes back many centuries. The purpose of it was to tell them why they were there: because, in medieval days, the King would normally govern with the assistance of the great Officers of State and his Privy Council. Only when something important happened in the life of the nation, such as a threat of war, was it considered necessary to bring together all the lords from the different parts of the country, which meant long and difficult journeys. The King had to 'show cause' why they had been summoned together in Parliament. And with them had to come the knights of the counties and the leading citizens of the towns—the Commons, in other words—because they were the ones who were going to have to vote money, through taxes, for the special purpose announced by the Crown. Nowadays, of course, Parliament meets pretty well all the time, because government concerns itself with more and more of the details of the lives of us all. But it is always useful to bear in mind the words of Edmund Burke about how far government should go in running affairs. He said:

> It is one of the finest problems in legislation, and what has often engaged my thoughts whilst I followed that profession,— what the state ought to take upon itself to direct by the public wisdom, and what it ought to leave, with as little interference as possible, to individual discretion. Nothing, certainly, can be laid down on the subject that will not admit of exceptions,— many permanent, some occasional. But the clearest line of distinction which I could draw, whilst I had my chalk to draw any line, was this: that the state ought to confine itself to what regards the state or the creatures of the state: namely, the exterior establishment of its religion; its magistracy; its revenue; its military force by sea and land; the corporations that owe their existence to its fiat; in a word, to everything that is *truly and properly* public,— to the public peace, to the public safety, to the public prosperity. In its preventive policy it ought to be sparing of its efforts. . . Statesmen who know themselves will, with the dignity which belongs to wisdom, proceed only in this the superior orb and first mover of their duty, steadily, vigilantly, severely, courageously: whatever remains will, in a manner, provide for itself. But as they descend from the state to a province, from a province to a parish, and from a parish to a private house, they go on accelerated in their fall. They *cannot* do the lower duty; and in proportion as they try it, they will certainly fail in the higher. They ought to know the different departments of things,—what belongs to laws, and what

manners alone can regulate. To these great politicians may give a leaning, but they cannot give a law.

When the Queen enters Parliament to open it, once a year, the scene is one of brilliance. At the head of the procession are the four Pursuivants, with their picturesque names—Rouge Croix, Blue Mantle, Rouge Dragon and Portcullis—wearing their tabards embroidered with the Royal Arms, followed by heralds and officers of the Court in full dress. The Comptroller and Treasurer of the Household carry white wands, the Private Secretary and the Keeper of the Privy Purse follow in their uniforms; after them come the Lord High Chancellor carrying the Great Seal, the Lord President of the Council, and two peers, one holding aloft the gold-sheathed Sword of State, the other the red velvet Cap of Maintenance trimmed with ermine. Then comes the Queen, in her ermine robe and wearing the Imperial Crown and many of the finest Crown Jewels.

As she enters the House of Lords the lights are turned up and the entire assembly rises to its feet. It is a brilliant gathering—peeresses in gowns of every hue, wearing tiaras, peers in their scarlet robes, archbishops, bishops and judges in their ceremonial robes and wigs, and the ambassadors of many other countries in their uniforms. When the Queen has taken her seat on the Throne she says: 'My Lords, pray be seated.'

Why is all this done? What is the purpose of this pageantry? It is, simply, to remind us of the holy mystery of government, reflecting the awe and majesty and brilliance of our Creator and of His Creation. Again, let us hear Edmund Burke:

> This consecration is made, that all who administer in the government of men, in which they stand in the person of God Himself, should have high and worthy notions of their function and destination; that their hope should be full of immortality; that they should not look to the paltry pelf of the moment, nor to the temporary and transient praise of the vulgar, but to a solid, permanent existence, in the permanent part of their nature, and to a permanent fame and glory, in the example they leave as a rich inheritance to the world.

When the Lords are seated, the Commons are summoned from their Chamber by the Gentleman-Usher of the Black Rod. The door of the House of Commons is closed against him; and he has to strike the door three times with his ebony rod. This ceremony dates back to the time when the Commons lived in fear of having the King's Messenger, Black Rod, come and interrupt their deliberations; and so they closed their doors against all comers, even members of the public, to show their independence and to assert their freedom to discuss, in peace, the affairs of the kingdom.

After Black Rod has rapped three times, the door is opened and he is allowed to proceed to the Bar of the House, which is a line beyond which only Members of Parliament are normally allowed to go. The Gentleman Usher of the Black Rod then advances to the Table of the House, bowing three times to Mr Speaker. He gives this message: 'The Queen commands this honourable House to attend Her Majesty immediately in the House of Peers.' The Speaker and the Members of the House then follow Black Rod to the House of Lords.

The Speaker, the Ministers of the Crown and Members of Parliament have to stand in a kind of pen, or box, at the end of the House of Lords, facing the throne, while the Queen reads the Speech from the Throne. Now the Queen is fully in Parliament with, assembled before her, all the branches of government of which she is the tree and the strength: first, the Lords, representing her Great Council of the Realm, together with the archbishops and bishops who tend the spiritual life of the nation; then the judges who declare the law; and the Commons who speak for the people.

This was the pattern of the medieval Parliaments. The Commons attended on the King in Parliament, heard what he wanted, and then went away by themselves to consider what support they could give. They have nearly always had their own room, or chamber, to which they could retire; and their freedom to state their grievances and to debate the money requirements of the King and his Council has become part of the constitution.

So, now, after hearing the Queen's Speech, the Commons

depart to their own House to discuss its contents. But before they do so, the Clerk of the House of Commons rises to give out the title of a Bill. It is always the same Bill, called the 'Outlawries Bill', and yet for nearly four hundred years it has never been passed into law. No-one wants it to become law because, quite simply, it just provides an excuse for the Commons to show their independence by attending to it before considering the business of the government.

On an ordinary day in the House of Lords the business is much the same as in the House of Commons. The lords do not wear their coronets and robes, just ordinary suits. They give three readings to each Bill, as in the Commons; for the House of Lords is the upper house and must also give its consent to a Bill before it can become an Act of Parliament. But debates in the House of Lords are likely to be quieter, less emotional, than in the Commons; and their rules reflect this difference. The Lord Chancellor, who is Speaker of the Lords, as well as being the foremost judge of the kingdom, sits on the woolsack in front of the throne to preside over debates. The woolsack is a kind of square couch packed with wool, for sheep-rearing was one of the great industries of this country, centuries ago. It is ironic that the Chancellor should sit on wool, for the enclosing of common land to rear sheep deprived many men of their basic living, and drove them from the land to the towns in search of work. The land enclosures produced much misery, poverty and crime, and their effects are still with us.

Unlike the Speaker of the Commons, the Lord Chancellor can join in a debate. When he does so, he must step aside from the woolsack, for the woolsack is not part of the House of Lords. That is because a Speaker of the House of Lords might not always be a peer: in which case he could not engage in debate. The word 'peer' comes from the Latin *pares*, meaning 'equal'. The peers are the equal of each other.

In many ways this is just a remnant of the past, when there were different orders of men, having different parts to play in the drama of the state. You may remember the quotation from King Alfred in Chapter 2 in which he said that the orders were: the men who pray, the men who fight and the men who work.

To that the oldest scriptures would add, the men who trade: so that it would become priests, soldiers (and rulers), traders and labourers. It was a question of status, of standing—and here again we are back to the Latin root which gives us such words as 'constitution', meaning 'standing together'. Unlike other animals, men stand up: and how they stand and where they stand are all-important to the work they have to do, as men. We speak of men standing upright and fearlessly. The power that is given to men to do anything at all useful in the community depends on the status we give them: so it is very important that we should give status to the right men. It is not much good asking a labourer to rule a country if he does not have the natural talent for it and has not been trained for the task.

It is one of the great purposes of a community that it should look for the natural talents of each individual and bring them out, by education, so that they can be used for the benefit of everyone. And when these talents and skills have been developed, the individual very naturally has the authority and the power to put them to good use. They may not necessarily be very big talents: never mind, so long as they are properly used, the individual should be respected for the work he does so well and given the opportunity and the materials he needs. Look back at that quotation from King Alfred and you will find that he says that it is a king's task to provide sustenance for his men (see page 15).

Working thus, a man's 'peers' are his equals: that is, other men who share the same work and have similar talents. We use the word 'peers' today to mean members of the House of Lords—but they are only peers in the sense that they have, or should have, the ability to govern sensibly and the training to perform that part.

Often enough, today, we get men and the parts they play terribly confused, and it is no wonder that nothing happens or the results are disturbing. A labourer is as good as a lord, it is said, so why should the lord have extra privileges and extra wealth? To that the answer must be, truly only if he needs them to carry out the very demanding work of governing the State.

Many members of the House of Lords have got their titles and their wealth and their lands from their forefathers; and many of them do not even bother to attend debates or concern themselves with the running of Parliament. That is why the House of Lords comes in for criticism, from time to time, and plans are made to change or even abolish it. You will hear it said that a number of lords only come to London when the House of Commons has passed a Bill which is directly contrary to their own selfish interests, and they want to vote against it in the House of Lords. But when there was last a major clash between the two Houses of Parliament, in 1911, a Parliament Act was passed into law which prevents the Upper House from dismissing the work of the Commons out of hand. All that the House of Lords can do now is return a Bill to the House of Commons with their suggestions for amendment—or the Lords might even reject it totally— but if the Commons insist, after a year, that they want the measure to go through, it can be presented to the Queen for her Royal Assent even if the Lords still refuse their consent. And if a Bill concerns only taxation or expenditure the Lords can hardly delay it at all.

A noble lord once said that the House of Lords exists 'to arrest the progress of such measures whenever we believe that they have been insufficiently considered and that they are not in accord with the deliberate judgment of the country'. He uses the word 'arrest'. That means to bring to a stop, to check, to delay. Sometimes the House of Commons, which is the emotional centre of government, sends up a Bill which is the result of hasty beliefs, fears or impatience; and then it is the duty of the Lords to say what is wrong with it and to return it for a time while more thought can be given to it. The word 'arrest' is a good one in this respect, because it signifies a temporary halt: it does not mean the end of the Bill, just time for reconsideration. Often enough that is all that is required; and the Bill, if the Commons still want it after thinking about it again, comes back to the Lords much improved.

We have said that debates in the House of Lords are quieter. Often they are wiser. The Speaker on his woolsack, the Lord Chancellor, does not have to keep order as his counterpart in the Commons has to do: indeed, the Lord Chancellor has very few powers. He does not decide which noble lord is going to speak next; nor can he tell them to shut up if they speak at great length. The lords are of equal standing, they are peers, and they behave courteously to each other. If it should be necessary to restore order to the House, it is open to any lord to rise and propose 'That the Clerk at the Table do read the Order of the House relating to asperity of speech'. That Order dates back to 1626 and runs as follows:

> To prevent misunderstanding, and for avoiding of offensive speeches, when matters are debating, either in the House or at Committees, it is for honour sake thought fit, and so ordered, that all personal, sharp, or taxing speeches be forborn, and whosoever answereth another man's speech shall apply his answer to the matter without wrong to the person; and as nothing offensive is to be spoken, so nothing is to be ill taken. . .

If you can imagine the wigged clerk standing up and reading all that (and more), you can readily understand that tempers cool by the time he has finished! Actually they are very fine words to describe conduct in debate. The number of times the Order has to be read amount to once or twice in a hundred years.

The high and intelligent level of debate in the House of Lords reflects its historic function as the Great Council of the Kingdom. Here you have gathered together some of the cleverest of men, representing the institutions: the Church, the law, universities, landowners, businessmen, trade unions and so on. They speak from long experience in their professions. Here the professions come together to share their wisdom in the common cause of good government. The House of Lords, therefore, has a vital part to play in ruling the nation.

There are at present just over a thousand peers, or lords. A quarter of that number are 'life peers': that is, they are appointed peers for their own lives only, and their sons and daughters cannot inherit the title after they have died. Every year the names of outstanding people are suggested to the Queen as being suitable for honours: and she usually accepts them for the grant of life peerages, or knighthoods, or membership of an order.

These life peers are the ones who are likely to attend the House and join in debates. Debates are not always only about Bills sent up from the Commons: they can be about any subject which touches on the interests of the nation. The lords have more time and freedom to discuss matters. They are not under the same pressures as Members of Parliament to 'get things done'. As a result they can give deeper and fuller attention to matters of great concern to the future of the country. Walter Bagehot said, 'Nobility is the symbol of mind': and here, if we did but realise it, is mind at work in the government of the nation. The House of Lords is not at all like the exciting and dramatic House of Commons: but in the House of Lords, at its best, there is a cool, reflective mind at work.

We have to be reminded, from time to time, that things are really quite different from what they seem to be. Most people are caught by the exciting shows going on in the House of Commons and think this is what government is all about. But the Commons are only part of the process of authority, which begins in stillness and quietness at the top, through the Queen, and reaches the people through the Lords and Commons. Members of Parliament are constantly having to look over their shoulders to see whether what they are saying and doing has the approval of the people who elect them. Yet elections, however important they are, are really only a way of seeing that authority is kept within bounds and is not abused.

Edmund Burke said: 'The people are the natural control on authority, but to exercise and control together is contradictory and impossible.' What this means is that the people do not have authority: it comes from above. But those exercising it always have to take into account the feelings of the people and not try to do things which the people cannot accept.

So the House of Lords is a very necessary part of our system of government. Not being elected, the peers are free from the hurly-burly of popular pressures and can give a long, straight look at the problems of the day. But they come in for criticism, mainly based on envy at the apparent wealth and privilege the lords seem to have. A lot of the criticism is directed at those lords—the majority—who do not come to Parliament very often. As we saw, this does not matter much, so long as there are men in the House who ably and wisely represent their professions.

Changes in the system are always being suggested, such as electing members of the House of Lords, or even doing away with them entirely. But the English constitution, not being a rigid, written thing, does of itself naturally grow and change. The House of Lords started off by being the Great Council of the King, where he could take the advice of his wise men and his warriors. These great men were given grants of land to sustain them while they served. They included, from the beginning, churchmen—bishops and abbots—because these were the learned people of the day. And the Council did not divide to hear law suits or to consider army matters: they did it all as one. Later, as government grew more complex and more people outside the clergy became educated, the offices and powers were divided up. Judges were appointed just to hear the people's grievances; Ministers and Secretaries of State came into being.

That left the House of Lords as an assembly of landowners: for the land which had originally been granted for services to the state was passed down through the families. Of course, many of these great families continued to train their sons to become servants of the King's Government. But others were greedy for land and took as much (and more) as they could control, either from the Church, when it was stripped of its lands in the sixteenth century, or from the people by way of enclosures. That certainly could not last: and, in 1911, came the clash between the landowners in the House of Lords and the Commons, mainly over the proposals by the Cabinet to tax the values of land. The result was, as we have seen, the Parliament Act, which took away the power of the landowners to stop legislation which was contrary to their selfish interests.

Since that time the House of Lords has changed. The introduction of the system of life peers has greatly increased the prestige and influence of the House, for these are men and women experienced in all walks of life. And so reform has taken place, quietly and gently. All that is necessary is for that reform to continue, and for the Queen's appointments to be the best possible. Violent alterations are not called for when the system is wisely developing itself.

9
The Church

> We know, and, what is better, we feel inwardly, that religion is
> the basis of civil society, and the source of all good, and of all
> comfort—*Edmund Burke*

These words of Edmund Burke, written at a time of peril for
the nation, express what we naturally feel about our
constitution. As we saw, the word 'constitution' means that by
which we stand together: and that is a firm faith in God. The
English nation is, at heart, deeply religious. We may not show
it very often: indeed, we are shy of speaking about it and many
of us do not go to church a great deal. But when there is a great
national event, such as the coronation of the Queen or her
Jubilee celebration, it is an act of devotion and of worship
made by us all.

The Church is an essential part of our system of
government. The Queen is Head of the Church of England. If
you look at a coin, you will see the Queen's head and beside it
the letters 'D.G. REG.F.D.' and the year. Those letters signify
Deo Gratia, Regina, Fidei Defensor—'By the Grace of God, Queen,
Defender of the Faith'. That is a good description of the natural
order: first of all, there is God, and it is by His Grace that we
have our system of government; then there is the Queen,
whose rule is utter service to the goodness which exists in men;
finally there is the faith of the people, which needs to be
maintained and defended.

Bracton, a wise old lawyer of the thirteenth century, virtually
established our constitution for us in these words, translated
from the Latin:

> The king has no equal within his realm. Subjects cannot be the
> equals of the ruler, because he would thereby lose his rule,
> since equal can have no authority over equal, nor a superior,

because he would then be subject to those subjected to him.
The king must not be under man but under God and the law,
because law makes the king. Let him therefore bestow upon the
law what the law bestows upon him, namely, rule and power,
for there is no *rex* [king] where will rules rather than *lex* [law] . . .
He is the vicar of God. And that he ought to be under the law
appears clearly in the analogy of Jesus Christ, whose viceregent
on earth he is, for though many ways were open to Him for His
ineffable redemption of the human race, the true mercy of God
chose this most powerful way to destroy the devil's work, he
would use not the power of force but the reason of justice. Thus
He willed Himself to be under the law that He might redeem
those who live under it. For He did not wish to use force but
judgement.

The King (or Queen), he says, is the vicar of God. 'Vicar' is a
word meaning someone who stands in place of. The Queen
stands in place of God, in an earthly sense. That is why we give
her so much respect and reverence. That does not mean to say
she is not human: of course not. Nor do we stop worshipping
God, and worship the Queen. But the Law of God, His Law for
creation, has to operate through persons: and, for this nation,
the Law comes through the Queen in Parliament, which is the
Sovereign.

What Bracton says is an echo of the Upanishads, the oldest
scriptures known to mankind:

. . . The king is above all men. The priest occupies a lower seat
at the coronation. The priest confers the crown upon the king,
is the root of the king's power.

Therefore though the king attain supremacy at the end of his
coronation he sits below the priest and acknowledges him as
the root of his power. So whoever destroys the priest, destroys
his root. He sins; he destroys the good. . .

Self created the good law. That law is the power of the king;
there is nothing higher than law. Even a weak man rules the
strong with the help of law; law and the king are the same. Law
is truth. Who speaks the truth, speaks the law; who speaks the
law, speaks the truth; they are the same.

And Plato says, much later, but still before our Christian era:

And when I call the rulers servants or ministers of the law, I
give them this name not for the sake of novelty, but because I
certainly believe that upon their service or ministry depends
the well- or ill-being of the state. For that state in which the law
is subject and has no authority, I perceive to be on the highway
to ruin; but I see that the state in which the law is above the
rulers, and the rulers are the inferiors of the law, has salvation,
and every blessing which the Gods can confer.

Thus it is most interesting to see that the basis of our
constitution was set down in ancient scriptures and in the
words of Plato.

You will note that, in the extract from the Upanishad,
mention is made of the priest conferring the crown upon the
king; but the king acknowledging the priest as the 'root of his
power'. So, at the coronation, which is a holy and mysterious
ceremony, the Archbishop of Canterbury anoints the Queen
and places the crown upon her head. But the Queen also
makes reverence to the Archbishop, for he is the priest, the
holy man of God.

At times of great danger—of moral crisis, which is the worst
kind of danger, when people do not know right from wrong—
it is the Archbishop's duty to speak and to lead. And,
traditionally, the two Archbishops, of Canterbury and York,
and some of the bishops have advised in the highest councils
in the land. They are members of the House of Lords. The
Archbishops are also Privy Councillors.

For many centuries the great offices of state were filled by
churchmen. They were councillors and judges and tax-
gatherers. The 'keeper of the king's conscience', the Lord
Chancellor, was a bishop: for the King had to have a priest to
turn to when his conscience was troubled, about what was the
right thing to do. 'Conscience' means 'together with knowledge',
and it was the Lord Chancellor's knowledge of the effects of
what the king wanted to do that was important.

Later, with the Reformation, when the Church of England
was established, the King grew less and less to rely on
churchmen for his officers of state. The Lord Chancellor
became, and still is, the foremost lawyer in the land. This all

reflected a growing apart of the ancient unity of Church and State: and for this reason people supposed that the Church should concern itself only with an individual's soul and his moral upbringing, and not with the great affairs of state.

Today, many countries (not this one) do not allow their leading churchmen to join in the assemblies and debates of government. Indeed, in the Communist states, the bishops and priests are prevented from saying anything at all to the people about the affairs of the country: but this is very difficult to prevent, and places like Russia and Poland are finding it increasingly so, because people naturally want the guidance and authority of their spiritual teachers. The duty of archbishops and bishops is to maintain a watch over human activities and to speak out when the chariot of the body of the nation is being drawn by the horses of senses down the road towards destruction. The Queen in Parliament is still the firm-footed charioteer; but she needs the wisdom, counsel ·and speech of her churchmen to assist her.

One of our greatest Archbishops, William Temple, said:

> The claim of the Christian Church to make its voice heard in matters of politics and economics is very widely resented, even by those who are Christian in personal belief and in devotional practice. It is commonly assumed that religion is one department of life, like art or science, and that it is playing the part of a busybody when it lays down principles for the guidance of other departments, whether art and science or business and politics.

Yet those same Christian principles are fundamental to everything we do and say, as individuals or as citizens of the State. No activity is without them. We cannot escape them. They lay down rules of conduct which govern us.

Sir William Blackstone, the judge who wrote the *Commentaries on the Laws of England*, said:

> Man, considered as a creature, must necessarily be subject to the laws of his creator, for he is entirely a dependent being. A being, independent of any other, has no rule to pursue, but such as he prescribes to himself; but a state of dependence will

inevitably oblige the inferior to take the will of him, on whom he depends, as the rule of his conduct: not indeed in every particular, but in all those points wherein his dependence consists. This principle therefore has more or less extent and effect, in proportion as the superiority of the one and the dependence of the other is greater or less, absolute or limited. And consequently, as man depends absolutely upon his maker for every thing, it is necessary that he should in all points conform to his maker's will.

This will of his maker is called the law of nature. For as God, when he created matter, and endued it with a principle of mobility, established certain rules for the perpetual direction of that motion: so, when he created man, and endued him with freewill to conduct himself in all parts of life, he laid down certain immutable laws of human nature, whereby that freewill is in some degree regulated and restrained, and gave him also the faculty of reason to discover the purport of those laws.

What are these great unchanging laws which govern everything we do and say? For us, in the Christian civilisation, there are essentially two, and they are stated in the Bible as follows:

Then one of them, which was a lawyer, asked him a question, tempting him, and saying,
Master, which is the great commandment in the law?
Jesus said unto him, Thou shalt love the Lord thy God with all thy heart, and with all thy soul, and with all thy mind.
This is the first and great commandment,
And the second is like unto it, Thou shalt love thy neighbour as thyself.
On these two commandments hang all the law and the prophets.

Notice that Our Lord does not say 'These are very good rules which you ought to practise some time'. He says they are commandments: you *shall* do them. And ever since then all the many laws under which we live have, as their strength, the force of those two simple commandments.

A wise French lawyer of the seventeenth century, Jean Domat, wrote:

However, although men have violated these fundamental laws, and although society be in a state strangely different from that which ought to be raised upon these foundations, and cemented by this union; it is still true, that these divine laws, which are essential to the nature of Man, remain immutable, and have never ceased to oblige men to the observance of them: and it is likewise certain . . . that all the laws which govern society, even in the condition in which it is at present, are no other than consequences of these first laws.

Of course, we do not find it easy just to observe those two commandments in all their simplicity. Loving God with all one's heart and soul and mind means being totally at His disposal to do whatever work He wills; loving one's neighbour as one's self means always seeing the goodness in others. But, to assist us, there are orders of law under which we live.

First, after the commandments, there is the Common Law. Plato said:

. . . and this is the sacred and golden cord of reason, called by us the common law of the State. . . Now we ought always to co-operate with the lead of the best, which is law. For inasmuch as reason is beautiful and gentle, and not violent, her rule must needs have ministers in order to help the golden principle in vanquishing the other principles.

The Common Law is based on reason. The light of reason, in the mind, shows us what is true and what is false, what is right and what is wrong. One needs to practise the use of reason. Plato speaks of the 'lead of the best' and of 'ministers': these are great men, great judges and statesmen and writers, who by their words show us what is reasonable, and people follow them. People may not know about the words these men have used; but they follow along the paths set down by these men. When they do, they do not come to harm. So these great men establish 'customs', rules of conduct, by which men live their everyday lives.

But if the Common Law fails, because of men's forgetfulness or wilfulness, then Statute Law steps in and lays down very precise measures for us to follow. Statute Law is the creation of

Parliament, as we have seen. And the word 'statute' is to do with 'standing': in this case, giving men the opportunity to stand and conduct themselves as men, if only they obey the stricter rules laid down by Parliament.

To give an example: many people drive on the roads today. The roads are crowded with cars. Now, if you drive your car simply and naturally, watching with great care for the interests of others, you are effortlessly following the Common Law principle 'to use reasonable care to avoid injuring those using the highway'. But if there are a lot of accidents, then plainly that duty is not being observed and Parliament sets down, in the Road Traffic Acts, strict rules as to what you can and cannot do with your car, including having it tested regularly and the condition of brakes and tyres, and so forth. All this is intended to do the same thing: to make sure that people obey the second commandment.

If people then start disobeying the will of Parliament, matters are very serious indeed. It is called 'anarchy', which is a word meaning 'without a chief'. You find 'arch' meaning 'chief' in words like 'archbishop', or chief bishop. But human nature cannot abide the loss of a ruling power, just as the body needs the mind to regulate it. So, where there is the breakdown of government in society, usually a strong leader arises to restore order. He is called a 'tyrant'. Then people must do exactly as they are told and all freedom vanishes. A tyrant can be brutal and his police and army will shoot and torture people to make sure they obey the leader. This is what happened in Hitler's Germany. It all comes about when men selfishly fail to carry out their duties towards each other. Often enough, under a tyranny, things seem to work very well indeed: trains run on time, roads and factories are built and the land is properly farmed. But people are made into slaves, for physical labour. They are not allowed to use their minds; to express themselves in words; to worship their Maker.

Fortunately, tyrannies do not last. They may cause untold misery for many years; but the spirit of Man cannot be confined for ever. Then people cast around for a different kind of leader, a spiritual man who will uplift them, free their minds and souls and give them good rules under which to live, and establish for them a system of government based on personal responsibility.

Our Lord Jesus came on earth at such a time, when there was a tyranny and when misery was widespread. By the example of his life and his teaching, and through the continuing work of His disciples, fresh hope and fresh civilisation were given to mankind. From that civilisation has arisen our own very fine constitution, which has been copied throughout the world, and which rests entirely on people observing their duties towards each other.

It is vitally important for the whole world that the English Constitution be maintained. Edmund Burke wrote:

> As long as you have the wisdom to keep the sovereign authority of this country as the sanctuary of liberty, the sacred temple consecrated to our common faith, wherever the chosen race and sons of England worship freedom, they will turn their faces towards you. The more they multiply, the more friends you will have; the more ardently they love liberty, the more perfect will be their obedience. Slavery they can have anywhere. It is a weed that grows in every soil. They may have it from Spain, they may have it from Prussia. But, until you become lost to all feeling of your true interest and your natural dignity, freedom they can have from none but you.

Burke was there reminding the House of Commons of the great tradition of liberty which runs in this country and of its importance as an example to the rest of the world. But the life and strength of the English Constitution are to be found in the two great commandments. That is why one great judge said: 'Christianity is parcel of the laws of England', meaning that to attack Christianity with evil words was to help destroy the foundation of our freedom.

Many people, even some in high places, have scoffed at the idea that Christianity is vital to our society. The House of Lords themselves, acting as the highest court of law in the land, once said: ' "Thou shalt love thy neighbour as thyself" is not part of our law at all.' That was in 1917, when disbelief in religion was strong.

Within fifteen years of that being said, a most curious thing happened. The highest judges in the country got themselves into a terrible tangle over a case of a girl who swallowed a snail from a ginger-beer bottle. They all wanted to help her, because she had been made ill through no fault of her own. But, as the judges saw the law at the time, there did not seem to be any remedy they could give her.

What happened was this. In about 1930 a girl was invited by a friend to go to a café where they decided to have ice cream and ginger beer. The friend paid for the ginger beer which came in a dark bottle which was opened at the table. The girl drank some of the ginger beer; the remainder was poured out into another glass and from the bottle came the remains of a dead snail. As a result the girl went to hospital with a serious illness.

Who was responsible for her illness? Who had a duty towards her not to treat her like this? Who should pay money to help her with hospital bills and her wages while she was away from work? The judges shook their heads. The owners of the café had not done anything wrong: they could not have seen a snail in such a dark bottle. The manufacturer of the ginger beer ought to be responsible: but the trouble was she had not paid for their product, her friend had, and the friend was not made ill. And, anyway, the bottle of ginger beer was not in itself a dangerous thing, like a gun; so that the manufacturer had taken as much care over making and selling it as anyone was entitled to expect. It looked as if the judges would have to say that it was all an unfortunate accident.

But Lord Atkin, a wise and great judge, went straight to the commandments for the law. He reminded everyone that 'the rule that you are to love your neighbour becomes, in law, you must not injure your neighbour'. That then gave the law a chance to step in, and to award damages where injury was caused. But who is my neighbour? Lord Atkin said it was someone who ought reasonably to have me in mind when doing or not doing something which affects me. For that reason the maker of the ginger beer owed a duty towards the girl which he had broken, and for which he must pay a penalty.

This one case is now the basis of the whole law of negligence. And now, whenever someone injures you, without really intending to, but very carelessly, the law will ask that question: Is he your neighbour? If he should have had you in mind when he did the act, then he is your neighbour and must help you now that you have been hurt.

Lord Atkin's words had a profound effect on the law. But all he really did was state the second commandment in a different form of words. And everyone accepts that this *is* the law, and always was.

So Christianity is central to our law and to our freedom. It is not a case of, wouldn't it be nice if we had some Christian principles in our government? The fact is they are there and are working.

10
The Universities

Where there is no vision, the people perish.—*Proverbs 29, v.18*

The universities are another branch of our government. As we saw, they are the places where ideas are studied that will rule the Cabinet and the House of Commons in years to come. Students at universities today will read and discuss ideas which will influence them greatly; and when they are older, and are perhaps in Parliament, they will try to put these ideas into practice. Since universities throughout the world teach what is fashionable at a particular time, you are likely to find that common ideas are at work in the governments of many different countries.

But what is a university? Looking in a dictionary, as we have done many times, we find that the word 'university' is made up from two Latin words meaning 'turning towards the one'. That is a very good description, because, however many subjects a university teaches, the whole purpose is to discover the truth, the one-ness of creation.

The poet Dryden wrote:

Happy the Man who, studying Nature's Laws,
Thro' known effects can trace the secret Cause.

What he is saying is that a man finds happiness in looking at the many objects around us, discovering the laws which formed those objects and going back to the one source from which all those laws sprang.

When you think of it, that is what mind is for, sorting out differences and relating everything to wholeness. When someone asks you the way to a particular street, you will find, if you are quick enough, that there is part of the mind which looks for the wholeness behind the question—where you are at the moment, where the other street is and what is the best way to get from one to the other—so as to give a truthful answer and make the other person happy.

If you, yourself, had at one time or other walked to the other street, and remembered the way, your answer would be based on knowledge. But if you could only describe the way, because someone else had told you, then your answer would be based on opinion. And, of course, it very much depends on whether the other person told you accurately, whether you listened carefully to all he said and whether you are now passing it on exactly, how the traveller gets on when he follows your directions.

Nations and governments need men of knowledge to guide them. Such men of knowledge are the authors of scriptures: the Upanishads, for example, or our own Bible. In the scriptures one finds the laws set down in writing, to guide everyone. But when it comes to stating what those laws mean, in everyday life, and establishing paths of conduct so that people do not get lost, nations and governments need to listen to men of true opinion. These are wise men, who have studied the great teachings, and are able to say what, in their opinion, is the best way forward. Sometimes people follow men who hold false opinions, have not studied the great teachings, or misinterpret them, and then there is trouble and confusion in the state, and injustice occurs. Plato said, about this:

> And now I can define to you clearly, and without ambiguity, what I mean by the just and unjust, according to my notion of them: When anger and fear, and pleasure and pain, and jealousies and desires, tyrannise over the soul, whether they do any harm or not,—I call all this injustice. But when the opinion of the best, in whatever part of human nature states or individuals may suppose that to dwell, has dominion in the soul and orders the life of every man, even if it be sometimes mistaken, yet what is done in accordance therewith, and the principle in individuals which obeys this rule, and is best for the whole life of man, is to be called just. . .

A good example of what Plato means is the life of Lord Denning, one of the greatest judges that this nation has ever produced. He was a judge for nearly forty years. He sat in the highest courts in the land, retiring in 1982, when he was eighty-three. So he had a wealth of experience to draw on: and his opinion of the law was likely to be true opinion, the opinion of the best. Lord Denning certainly did all he could to make sure that 'anger and fear and pleasure and pain and jealousies and desires' did not cloud his judgment, and therefore he gave justice to the people. Ordinary people loved and respected and listened to him. They obeyed him. For they knew that he spoke with authority.

When he was eighty years old, and still sitting daily as the leading judge in the Court of Appeal, he wrote a book called *The Discipline of Law*. On his birthday he sat in a bookshop personally signing copies of his book. The queue of people outside, waiting for hours to approach Lord Denning, stretched all the way up the street. The queue consisted mainly of young people, law students. Whenever Lord Denning spoke to students, the hall was packed. This is a healthy sign: for young people do not always listen patiently to their elders. But, in Lord Denning, they recognised truth at work.

This great judge came from a humble family, living in a country town. Of three brothers, one became an admiral, one a general and the third, Lord Denning, a judge. His strength and his knowledge are derived from Christianity, and Lord Denning is a devout man. Once he wrote that justice 'is not something you can see. It is not temporary but eternal. How does man know what is justice? It is not the product of his intellect but of his spirit. The nearest we can get to defining justice is to say that it is what the right-minded members of the community—those who have the right spirit within them—believe to be fair.'

So there are great ideas, based on knowledge, at work in society. Indeed, there must be all the time: for 'Where there is no vision, the people perish'. That means that people must always be given a view of themselves in relation to their Creator. The Bible says that God created Man in his own image. That image is most important to everyone, because without it they would have no real reason for existence. So a mirror has to be held up for people to look into and see themselves as a reflection of God. From time to time the vision has to be renewed, because the old mirror becomes cloudy and distorted. It is the work of thinkers in universities, and writers and artists, to hold up a new mirror every so often in the history of mankind. When they do so it is called a renaissance, a rebirth.

Have a look at a medieval painting. It comes from a bygone age, perhaps seven or eight hundred years ago. To our eyes it looks all wrong: some of the people in it are very big and others very small. Most medieval painting has a religious purpose, and the important figures in it, Jesus, say, or Mary, dominate the scene. All the others are scaled down in size. But that was how people living at the time saw themselves: they were all related to each other, and to God, in a natural order of importance, from the lowest working in the fields, through the lords and the king, to the saints and Our Lord.

Now look at a drawing by Leonardo da Vinci, one of the world's greatest artists, who lived in Italy in about 1500. We are looking at things as we see them today: people are the same size and, if we look closely, we will see how immensely detailed the drawing is. Leonardo made many sketches of the bone structures of human beings and animals. He was fascinated by how things worked; and he was capable of designing many inventions which we take for granted today, such as aeroplanes. It is as though the grand design of our lives now was set down in these drawings, nearly five hundred years ago. And this is how we see ourselves today: we are very concerned with the smallest details. In science we look for the smallest particles. It is, of course, only another way of worshipping God in creation, to express wonder and awe at the beauty and skill of His creatures.

What happened in between these two views, the medieval one of men in all their relationships building up to God, and the modern view of the individual as a very fine instrument? Well, visions do fade; mirrors do grow cloudy and distorted. As people lost trust in the medieval sense of unity, the effects showed themselves in the body of the Church itself, which grew old and crumbled and was struck with disease. It was time for a new renaissance, a rebirth, a new vision of Man.

When these things happen, there have to be farsighted and compassionate men, concerned about the future wellbeing of mankind. They work at a high level, indeed. But they work with ideas, and through the use of words to express these ideas. In terms of our present culture, which came from the Renaissance in the city of Florence in Italy in the late 1400s, we owe much to the work of a man called Marsilio Ficino and the Academy of Learning which he founded in that city. He it was who inspired artists to portray the new vision.

Ficino loved the writings of Plato. He translated them from Greek into Latin so that they could be read and studied by the scholars of the time. He wrote letters to important people throughout Europe, among them our own Dean Colet, Dean of St Paul's Cathedral and founder of St Paul's School, which still exists. By his efforts, there was a re-awakening of all the many skills and talents of which mankind is capable. The results of all this are described by the historian, J.R. Green:

> The world was passing through changes more momentous than any it had witnessed since the victory of Christianity and the fall of the Roman Empire. Its physical bounds were suddenly enlarged. The discoveries of Copernicus revealed to man the secret of the universe. Portuguese mariners doubled the Cape of Good Hope and anchored their merchant fleets in the harbours of India. Columbus crossed the untraversed ocean to add a New World to the Old. Sebastian Cabot, starting from the port of Bristol, threaded his way among the icebergs of Labrador. This sudden contact with new lands, new faiths, new races of men quickened the slumbering intelligence of Europe into a strange curiosity. . . . The capture of Constantinople by the Turks, and the flight of its Greek scholars to the shores of Italy, opened anew the science and literature of the older world at the very hour when the intellectual energy of the Middle Ages had sunk into exhaustion. The exiled Greek scholars were welcomed in Italy, and Florence, so long the home of freedom and of art, became the home of an intellectual revival. The poetry of Homer, the drama of Sophocles, the philosophy of Aristotle and of Plato woke again to life beneath the shadow of

the mighty dome with which Brunelleschi had just crowned the
City by the Arno. All the restless energy which Florence had so
long thrown into the cause of liberty she flung, now that her
liberty was reft from her, into the cause of letters.

What do you notice about that rather long extract? It seems,
does it not, to be full of that same restless energy which he
describes in his last sentence. It is a kind of explosion of
human energy, resulting in new discoveries everywhere. But it
came out of nothing new: it came, really, from re-finding all
the wealth of knowledge stored in the books of men of ideas
who lived many centuries before then. And a renaissance is
usually like that. It means that much work has to be done
beforehand, translating and understanding the words of the
wise, from a long time ago, so as to refresh and restore human
effort.

We are still making discoveries, based on the impulse of the
Renaissance in Florence. But, perhaps, the impulse is
beginning to run down: it has been going now for nearly five
hundred years. In due course a new vision will be required.
For the trouble with the present one is that, as time goes on,
the thinkers and the writers and the artists get it wrong. They
are still under its influence, as far as their methods of working
go; but they begin to forget its purpose, which is to glorify God
in Creation.

All the beautiful detail which Leonardo showed in the
human body, in order to praise God's work, becomes worship
of the body itself. We see that happening now, where people
are more concerned about their bodies and their cars and
houses than they are about their spirit.

The earliest universities, such as Oxford and Cambridge in
this country, were centres to which students flocked in order to
hear the masters expound their ideas. A really brilliant speaker
would gather round him students from all over Europe. And
the students themselves, as they advanced through their
'degrees', or levels of ability to teach, were required to speak
and to debate with each other. Teaching was largely by word of
mouth, at a time when books were hard to come by. Students

of law, for example, in their Inns of Court, which were like universities, learned their subject by listening to the best judges of the time, at work in their courts; making notes of what they heard and then practising to speak and argue cases in mock trials, or 'moots', after dinner in the hall of their Inn. Some of the notes taken by students make the earliest record we have of judgments in court, which have helped to guide other judges afterwards.

This tradition of teaching by the spoken word, rather than just reading books, is most important. We still have it, of course, in our universities and schools. When something is written down it tends to become fixed, and rigid; but a good teacher or lecturer knows what his audience needs to hear and can deal with their questions. Thus the subject remains lively and interesting.

Some of the best books we read nowadays were originally lectures or discussions or speeches, given to audiences. Plato's work, for example, consists of his record of what Socrates and those around him said. Indeed, our New Testament is a record of what Jesus said and did, and not of what he wrote down. The wise words of Edmund Burke come to us in the form of speeches which he made to the House of Commons: and those words are still being quoted out loud and are still helping to govern the nation.

Sir William Blackstone gave a series of lectures at the University of Oxford in the eighteenth century, which were later to be published as his *Commentaries on the Laws of England*. The most striking features of the *Commentaries* today are the beauty and measure of the language, and the sense of reason which fills the whole work. This is the kind of work which has to be done, from time to time, to collect together our tradition and remind people what they stand for: their 'constitution', in other words. When Blackstone spoke, the Common Law of England was not well known: it had become a mystery and an old, creaking, gloomy machine which served only the lawyers themselves. Law students sensed how ridiculous and meaningless it was all becoming: they got riotous and threw bread rolls and beer tankards even at the judges.

So Blackstone knew he had to open up the subject, and let the great light of reason in on the darkness surrounding the principles of Common Law. This he did by carefully explaining every point and showing the reason behind it, in majestic prose. He loved to read Shakespeare. This is a very good practice and training for speaking and writing, to study the works of the greatest poets and to appreciate their command of language.

For law comes to us through language. Ideas are expressed in words; and they make us do things. If the words are fine and well chosen, it is likely that they will lead us in the right direction. There is no doubt in people's minds what they mean. The best law, that which takes us back to our own true happiness, can always be expressed simply, clearly and directly. For example, read this:

Whatever we see in society that is contrary to order, is a natural consequence of the disobedience of Man to the first Law, which commands him to love God. For this Law being the foundation of the second, which enjoins men to love one another; Man could not violate the first of these two Laws, without falling at the same time into a state which hath carried him to a breach also of the second Law, and consequently to disturb the order of society.

The first Law was to unite men in the possession of the Sovereign Good: and they found in that Good two perfections which were to make their common happiness: one, that it is capable of being possessed by all persons; and the other, that it may be the entire happiness of everyone in particular. But Man having transgressed the first Law, and having gone astray from the true happiness, which he could find nowhere but in God alone, he hath sought after it among sensible Goods, in which he found two defects opposite to these two characters of the Sovereign Good; one, that these Goods cannot be possessed by all; and the other, that they cannot make the happiness of anyone.

These words were not written by Blackstone. They are the words, in translation, of a French lawyer, Jean Domat, who lived in the century before Blackstone. Yet they are very clear and simple words; they are reasonable; they do not cause doubt and confusion. Words like these quieten and refresh the mind. They are truthful.

So the universities, at their best, are places where the finest ideas of mankind are studied, conveyed in the finest language. When this happens, men and women who take part in the government of the nation have good, clear minds and are able to speak with authority, so that there is no doubt what is required of people. But when universities teach false opinions, which always have to be expressed in long, difficult words, it is no wonder that governments are torn by doubt and the people are fearful.

A Member of Parliament once said:

> Whether it be in politics, philosophy, religion or anything else, the one cardinal characteristic of truth is simplicity. The greatest truth that man ever heard was spoken in the language of simplicity in the streets of Jerusalem. Simplicity and truth stand together, and whenever you get into complexity beware, because there is a falsity somewhere.

11
The Law Courts: 1

Long experience, and many trials of what was best for the common good, did make the Common Law.—*Sir John Davies*

If people behaved naturally, and did what was right, there would be very little need for government by other men. The plain fact is, when people do not want to know what their duties are, and avoid them, other people have to tell them what to do and how to do it. Then you have kings and ministers and parliaments and policemen. It all becomes complicated, with lots of men telling you what you have to do, when, really, each individual has the knowledge of right and wrong within him.

Look at the Book of Samuel in the Bible. This tells you that the ancient nation of Israel had judges to look after them, before they ever had kings. Samuel was the last of the judges, who lived about a thousand years before Our Lord was born. His name, Samuel, means 'heard of God': and you may remember, if you have read the story, how he was given as a child into the service of the temple and of the priests; and how the Lord called him three times during the night and each time he ran to the priest, Eli, saying 'Here am I', thinking the priest had called him. Then Eli told Samuel to reply, 'Speak, Lord; for thy servant heareth'. And God chose to speak through Samuel to the Israelites.

In Chapter 2 of the Book of Samuel, verse 25, it says:

If one man sin against another, the judge shall judge him; but if a man sin against the Lord, who shall intreat for him?

This means that at the time the Israelites walked in the ways of the Lord their God, and accepted His commandments, as given to them by their priests. They also had judges, wise men who could solve any disputes which arose between them; but essentially they were God-fearing and law-abiding.

However, when Samuel grew old, the people came to him and said they wanted a king to rule over them. This signifies that they were unwilling to rule themselves, and wanted someone strong and powerful to stand between them and God, to take on the responsibility for their actions. We get a sense of this, even today, in the coronation service when the Queen is dedicated, or given to God, on behalf of the nation, to reign over us: but also to take responsibility for our affairs. We pray: 'God save the Queen.' She thus becomes the 'firm-footed charioteer' in the chariot of the nation. Nevertheless we should never forget that there is a 'firm-footed charioteer' in the chariot of everyone's body; and if we obeyed him we should need outside government less and less.

But the Israelites were becoming lazy and idle, and they told Samuel that they wanted a king to do the work for them, in the way that other nations had kings. This troubled Samuel and he prayed to the Lord.

> And the Lord said unto Samuel, Hearken unto the voice of the people in all that they say unto thee; for they have not rejected thee, but they have rejected me, that I should not reign over them.

Samuel told the Israelites what having a king would mean to them: a king might enslave them, he might take away their money and property, he might reward his officers at their cost. Indeed if we look at the history books, we find that the words of Samuel have often come true: people have exchanged their freedom, which is the freedom to do good, for the ruthless rule of strong kings. When William the Conqueror came to this country, in 1066, he enslaved the people and gave their lands to his cronies, simply because the people were tired and unwilling to fend for themselves. Sir William Blackstone describes what it was like to live under the earliest Norman king:

> The nation at this period seems to have groaned under as absolute a slavery as was in the power of a warlike, an ambitious, and a politic prince to create. . . The law, too, as well as the prayers, were administered in an unknown tongue. The

ancient trial by jury gave way to the impious decision by battle.
The forest laws totally restrained all rural pleasures and manly
recreations. And in cities and towns the case was no better; all
company being obliged to disperse, and fire and candle to be
extinguished, by eight at night, at the sound of the melancholy
curfew.

This description would fit, almost word for word, what the
tyrant Hitler did to the countries of Europe that he conquered
forty years ago, and also to what the Russians have done, in the
name of Communism, since then. But in this country, in the
1940s, there was a great sense of personal responsibility for the
freedom that was threatened, and a desire to fight, if need be,
against the forces of evil. The people woke up and, with one
accord, went to war to protect their freedom to rule
themselves.

As we know, from the Book of Samuel, the Israelites would
not listen to Samuel when he warned them about giving up
their personal rule, under God, for the rule of kings.

Nevertheless the people refused to obey the voice of Samuel;
and they said, Nay; but we will have a king over us;
That we also may be like all the nations; and that our king may
judge us, and go out before us, and fight our battles.

It is those last few words that are so interesting: what the
Israelites are saying is that they want a king to fight their battles
for them. They do not want to do it for themselves. They are
giving up, surrendering, their own freedom to do right for the
direction and authority of a king who may, or may not, abuse
them.

At a later stage of history, when the Romans conquered
almost all the known world, they had a maxim in their Latin
tongue: *Quod principi placuit legis habet vigorem, cum populus ei et in
eum omne suum imperium et potestatem conferat.* This says, in effect,
that law is what the prince (or king) says it is, for the people
have given him their authority and power. This can be a very
dangerous notion, in the wrong hands: it can lead to tyranny.
Yet it expresses what the Israelites had done, by giving up their
duties and responsibilities towards one another, in exchange

for the rule of a king. As we have seen, our own great lawyer, Bracton, in the thirteenth century, was very careful to say that this was not so, as far as England was concerned: for here 'The king must be under no man, but under God and the law, for the law makes the king'. The king must obey the law which the people have accepted as their way of life.

Many countries on the continent of Europe have accepted Roman Law as the basis of their constitutions. They did this long ago, because they were unwilling to observe the duties on which personal freedom is founded, and hence wanted someone strong at the centre of government to tell them what to do. The Common Law of the English nation is totally different from the Roman Law: every Englishman is free to do and think and say whatever he likes, so long as he does not offend or injure another. Under the rigid, written constitutional laws of other European nations, individuals are given only certain rights to do and say certain things, and these are subject to what the authorities dictate.

This country is now a member of the European Economic Community, which is really a big market-place for the goods produced in the various states. Yet the European Economic Community is based on the Roman Law way of looking at things, with a strong central authority of a few men making all the decisions. There is a European Parliament; but it is not at all like the Parliament we have in this country, and has few real powers. It may be that this will change, over the years, with men and women from this country going to the European Parliament to represent us there, and making sure that the principles learned at Westminster are put to work, mainly by asking questions and ensuring full debate, so that the few men at the centre are brought under 'God and the law'. Blackstone says:

> . . . It is one of the characteristic marks of English liberty, that our common law depends on custom; which carries this internal evidence of freedom along with it, that it probably was introduced by the voluntary consent of the people.

What is 'custom'? Skeat's *Etymological Dictionary* tells us that the word 'custom' comes from two Latin words, *cum*, meaning 'together, greatly, very' and *suus*, meaning 'one's own'. This is very important to an understanding of custom, because it implies all of us being true to that which we all own, which is ourselves. It is a matter of conduct, which really means how much care we take of the Self which travels in the chariot of the body, always present with the firm-footed charioteer. 'Conduct', in fact, meant 'escort' originally; and it is how we escort the Self on our journey through life that is significant. That Self is the presence of God. It is always there and always accessible. But we should treat it as an honoured guest, and not do or say anything which would make us ashamed in its presence.

Good custom therefore leads the people safely and honourably through life. It makes them observe their duties towards one another. To the extent that good custom rules, there is little or no need for statutes or regulations and government officials. The people will conduct themselves. They may not realise that they are under law: but they will say 'We have been doing it like this for generations and it has been good for us'. Probably they would not be able to tell you how and why the custom began; but it is passed on, by example, from parents to children.

Good custom is the Common Law. That is, it is the law common to the people. It is all their own. It truly belongs to them. And Common Law, custom, is based on reason. Plato said: '. . . and this is the sacred and golden cord of reason, called by us the common law of the State.'

Sir John Davies, Attorney-General for Ireland, wrote in 1612:

> For a Custom taketh beginning and groweth to perfection in this manner: When a reasonable act once done is found to be good and beneficial to the people, and agreeable to their nature and disposition, then do they use it and practise it again and again, and so by often iteration and multiplication of the act it becometh a custom; and being continued without interruption time out of mind, it obtaineth the force of a Law.
>
> And this Customary Law is the most perfect and most excellent, and without comparison the best, to make and

preserve a Commonwealth. For the written Laws which are made either by the Edicts of Princes, or by Councils of Estates, are imposed upon the Subject before any trial or probation made, whether the same be fit and agreeable to the nature and disposition of the people, or whether they will breed any inconvenience or no. But a Custom doth never become a Law to bind the people, until it hath been tried and approved time out of mind, during all which time there did thereby arise no inconvenience: for if it had been found inconvenient at any time, it had been used no longer, but had been interrupted, and consequently it had lost the virtue and force of a Law.

Here is where the judges come in, for they are reasonable men, and they establish customs for the people to follow. So, in the Book of Samuel, we learn that judges came first and kings after. When the Israelites would no longer obey the judges, and follow the paths of good conduct laid down for them, they had to have kings whose 'written laws' and 'edicts' would direct them, whether it suited them or not.

There is a lesson in this for us. For, in this nation, we are justly proud of the Common Law, which is a gentle law. Plato says as much: '. . . there are other [laws] which are hard and of iron, but this one is soft because golden . . . For inasmuch as reason is beautiful and gentle, and not violent, her rule must needs have ministers in order to help the golden principle in vanquishing the other principles.' It is gentle because if we just observe our duties towards each other—loving our neighbours as ourselves—then we do not even know the law is at work. It happens naturally, and we are led to our own real happiness.

But we must observe the duties. And we must respect and obey the judges. They are men who give careful thought to what is proper conduct for the people. Although a judge is concerned with a particular dispute which is brought to his attention, he knows that his judgment will affect the way people act in similar situations afterwards. He makes his judgment in the light of reason. And he is helped and guided in this by what other judges have decided in the past. It is a continuing process, with each judge adding his contribution until there is, quite clearly, a custom which the people will not go against. Chief Justice Coke once said:

> . . . if all the reason that is dispersed into so many several heads were united into one, yet could he not make such a law as the law in England is; because by many successions of ages it hath been fined and refined by an infinite number of grave and learned men, and by long experience grown to such a perfection, for the government of this realm, as the old rule may be justly verified of it. . . . No man out of his own private reason ought to be wiser than the law, which is the perfection of reason.

You will remember that, in Chapter 9, we spoke about the famous case in which a girl was poisoned by drinking ginger beer which had a dead snail in it. Lord Atkin, one of the judges in that case, recalled the great principle of loving your neighbour as yourself, and said that the girl was reasonably a neighbour of the manufacturer of the ginger beer—even though they had never met and lived miles apart from each other—because the manufacturer must have known that someone like her would open the dark bottle and drink its contents, without being able to see that there was a snail inside. In doing so, Lord Atkin looked back in the Law Reports to see what other judges had said before him: they had certainly decided that when a thing was dangerous in itself, like a gun, a manufacturer had to be extra careful about its safety. Lord Atkin took the next step in reason and said that even though a bottle of ginger beer is not, in itself, dangerous, it can become so if the manufacturer is careless about the purity of its contents: in which case he is liable if someone is injured. Likewise he took another step in reason when he found that judges in the past had said that a duty of care arose when two people or their property were close to each other: Lord Atkin took the commandment and said that being a neighbour did not just mean living next door, but anyone who reasonably would be affected by what I did was close to me, and I had to take care not to harm them. Thus, said Lord Atkin, 'the law in this matter as in most others is in accordance with sound common sense'.

The result of this judgment has been that makers of all the many products we buy and consume know that they have to inspect and pack their goods carefully. The custom has grown up of having people in the factory just checking goods to see whether there are any defects and making sure there are no impurities. Even if they have never heard of the snail-in-the-ginger-beer-bottle case, manufacturers know that they are required to act responsibly. It is the custom.

The decision in this case has had a very great effect in reminding everyone of their duties towards each other. And, since then, the judges have been 'fining and refining' the law to cover other situations where people are expected to act as neighbours. For instance, very recently, a little boy was playing in a field with his brothers. There was a path through the field leading towards an electric railway line. The railway line was, of course, fenced off; but the fence was broken down, and the British Railways Board had known about it for some time but had not done anything about it. The boy climbed through the gap in the fence, went on to the line and was severely burned by the electric current.

Now the British Railways Board said they were not responsible for the injury because the little boy should not have been there: he was a trespasser. Even though the fence was broken, he had no right to go on to the land carrying the railway line. They claimed that judges in the past had decided that no-one owed a duty of care towards a trespasser, even if he was a small boy who did not know what trespassing meant, because otherwise it would be extremely difficult and expensive to keep out everyone. But the high judges of the House of Lords did not agree: they said that the British Railways Board were liable for the injuries caused. A wrongdoer— because trespassing is wrong—could still be a neighbour, for he was a human being and there was a common duty of humanity: so that when a powerful body like British Rail knew that children played near their line they had to be especially careful to see that their fences were in good repair. Of course, they would not be required to do more than that: if children actually climbed up and over a six-foot high fence, for example, and dropped on to the electric line, that would not be the fault of the British Railways Board. But ordinary humanity, care and forethought for others, especially children, made good fencing a necessity. So by reason, the judges were again establishing a custom to be followed wherever a big company has dangerous equipment on its land.

Another example of good custom which has been established by reason is the judgments of the judges themselves, given in open court before anyone who cares to attend. There is no law written down somewhere requiring judges to give reasons in public for deciding a case one way or the other: but they do. No-one quite knows when that custom started—it is very old, and may have begun when a great king, Henry II, sent out royal judges to ride on horseback from town to town, listening to the complaints of the people. This was an act of great care on the part of the king, for the people learned to trust and rely on the wisdom of the fine men—the itinerant, or travelling, justices as they were called—whom the king sent out to do justice in his name. The Common Law developed from their work, for they gave customs, good ways of conduct, for people to live by. They established these customs through reason in their judgments. Whenever gentle reason is spoken, men want to listen and to follow. And still, nearly nine centuries later, the Judges of the Queen's Bench in their red robes travel round the country: only, these days, they do not go on horseback.

So this in itself is nothing else than a custom: the judges giving reasons why they decide a particular case in a certain way. You can go any day of the week during a 'Law Term' to the Royal Courts of Justice in the Strand and see the judges at work. Perhaps you will hear them deliver judgment. It is a rule that these judgments have to be spoken out loud, in public; for, if what is said does not sound right it is not reasonable. It is a very good test for anyone to have to state their reasons by word of mouth: and, if the voice sounds false, you can be pretty sure that the words spoken do not come from the wholeness of reason.

There is another thing: when judgments are spoken in words they can be examined by judges in the higher courts. If they are shown to be wrong, judges in the Court of Appeal or, at the highest level, the House of Lords, can correct them. All judges can make mistakes from time to time: perhaps they might let personal likes or dislikes cloud their minds. When this happens, it is always good to know that there are even more experienced men sitting in courts above them, to whom one can appeal. And so justice emerges from the reason 'that is dispersed into so many several heads', as old Judge Coke put it. You will remember he said: 'No man out of his own private reason ought to be wiser than the law, which is the perfection of reason.'

Imagine what it would be like to live in a country—and there are such countries in the world today, as there have been in the past—where judges are not required to state their reasons! Where a single judge is all-powerful, and can do what he likes, without being asked to tell you why he is doing it. This is tyranny. Under tyranny, men can be sent to prison or to death without being told why.

Such is the love of freedom in this country that if a man is locked up, against his will, without good and sufficient reason for his detention, judges will order that he be set free immediately. This is called *Habeas Corpus*, which literally means let us have his body out of confinement. It is considered so important that, if a wigged and gowned barrister stands up in court and says, 'My Lord, I have an application which concerns the liberty of the subject', the judge must put everything else aside and hear him.

Slavery exists in the world today as it has done in the past. Communist Russia is one of the worst offenders, for millions of Russians live in prison camps and work hard with no freedom and very little food. English merchants were also guilty, in the past, of enslaving Africans and shipping them to America to work on the cotton plantations. It took many years of patient effort to change the idea that such an evil trade was necessary.

In 1771 a black man was held in chains on board a ship lying in the Thames. The famous judge Lord Mansfield declared his detention to be unlawful. 'The air of England is too pure for any slave to breathe,' he said. 'Let the black go free': and he was freed.

12
The Law Courts: 2

I do swear by Almighty God that I will do right to all manner of people after the laws and usages of this Realm without fear or favour, affection or ill-will.—*Oath sworn by judges on appointment*

What are judgment and reason, by which a judge comes to know how to do right?

Reason, we have said, is a light which shines in the mind and shows the right path ahead. Judgment is the minister, or servant, of reason. It is a kind of sifting-out process by which all that is unnecessary is put aside, and one or two real questions are left for intellect to answer. If the sifting-out is done well, then the real questions often answer themselves, in the light of reason. The mind says it is obvious; it stands to reason. One answer is truthful; the other untruthful. One way is right; the other is wrong.

When there is a quarrel between two people they often cannot tell right from wrong because their own feelings cloud the issues. Then they may go to solicitors, who are lawyers who deal first of all with the public. They will describe the facts of the dispute, as well as they can remember them; and the solicitors, one for each of them, will ask questions in order to sort out the important facts. It may be that, at this point, it will become evident where the truth lies; and the solicitor will say 'Well, you promised to do this and this; you have broken your promise; and you really ought to make amends to the other person'. Always it is important that the man himself comes to recognise the justice of the situation, so that he does not go away bearing a grudge.

Freeing a man from the grudge he bears is the way of justice and judgment. Words such as these bear the imprint of the old Sanskrit syllable *yu*, meaning 'to bind, to join together'. The purpose is to reunite men, to bring them together again, to remind them of their essential unity. Quarrels and disputes divide men; and it is the purpose throughout the legal process to make men see, through reason, what is the right thing to do, so that they may be united again.

In fact, men ought to come to the resolution of their disputes themselves: they may need the assistance of trained lawyers to help clarify their minds, but only when a grudge is deep-seated ought it to come before the courts for determination. Lawyers sometimes say that they have failed if a case they are dealing with gets as far as the courts; for they are constantly endeavouring to get their clients to agree, in a way which satisfies all of them.

The next stage, if there is no agreement, is for the solicitor to submit the matter to a barrister for his opinion. Barristers cannot meet the public directly; they have to work through solicitors, who bring them cases. The reason for this is, again, the process of sifting, of judgment. The solicitor tries to clarify the dispute between the parties by writing down all the facts, as he understands them, in a document called a 'brief to Counsel', which is then tied up with pink ribbon and sent to a barrister, also known as counsel. The barrister will read the papers; he may call for further documents or he may want to see the client himself, in order to form an opinion of what the law is in that particular situation. Again, the barrister is exercising judgment. He may throw the light of his reason and experience on the problem and, hopefully, that light will show clearly to the parties involved what they have to do which is right for both of them—and which they both accept as being right, because reasonable.

Barristers are men and women who stand up for people in the courts and speak for them. They wear wigs and gowns when they are in court: if you look carefully you will see that a barrister's gown has a kind of pocket hanging from the back. In the old days his client would slip some money in the pocket while the barrister's back was turned if he liked the way the barrister spoke for him and argued his case. Still, today, the money that you pay for having a barrister speak for you is considered to be a gift, and not payment for the services he has given. He would still have to speak for you even if you did not pay him. This is the relic of an old tradition of service: that a man's talents for speech and reasoning are not his own, but come to him from God and must be used in the common service of humanity. It was true also in the old days for teaching: a man could not be paid for teaching knowledge that was not his, but the common wealth of all men. Such knowledge could be received by all men who made the effort to learn; but it was not to be trapped and held on to, but passed on for the benefit of others. Nevertheless, the teacher (and the barrister) was to be maintained, and given what was necessary for his livelihood: his food, clothing, books, accommodation. You will remember that King Alfred spoke about this.

If the matter is to go further on its journey towards the courts, the barrister will have to draw up what are called 'pleadings'. Here, again, judgment is required: for the pleadings state, as concisely as possible, what is the nature of the dispute between the parties. Only those issues on which there is still disagreement are written down for the judge to decide. In that process, if the barrister cannot find the words to describe the claim that is being made, or if his pleadings do not sound right, it is a pretty good sign that the claim is a weak one and should be abandoned or settled before the parties go to all the expense of having their days in court.

People complain about the cost of going to court, and some say that a law suit will be won by those rich enough to afford going to the highest courts: hence the state will now pay, through legal aid, for someone who has been done an injustice but is too poor to meet the expense. But there is perhaps merit in not making it too easy for someone to approach the judges. People will then try to resolve their own difficulties, or even think twice about getting into arguments with their neighbours in the first place: which is the best and most peaceful of solutions. After all, the best form of government is self-government, in which you do not have to rely on others to tell you what is right and wrong. Of course, in the end, if a dispute is incapable of solution between the parties there ought to be access to the courts: but it should be a last resort and not the first thing that comes to people's minds, so that the courts are clogged with unnecessary actions.

Sometimes the only way to settle a problem is to have it discussed in court, before a judge. Both sides have counsel to speak for them and, while they are arguing the case, it may become apparent to everyone in court what the answer is. The same mental processes as before go on; the facts are sifted and the important questions emerge, but this time the voice is added, and one can *hear* when an argument is right. A good judge is one who listens with attention and says very little, except to ask an occasional question to clarify the issues. Some judges say that the hardest thing they had to learn when they became judges was to sit still and remain quiet: but it is the quiet mind which is needed, if the right answer is to come. There is a Latin maxim which says *Ex facto jus oritur*, meaning 'the law arises out of the fact'. If the judge is told all that is relevant to the dispute between the parties, he will often know—quite suddenly—what the law is. And it will be simple and direct and will make commonsense.

This again is an example of watching from stillness, which we saw in the Queen. It is very powerful, for it sorts out the tangles and gives direction. Often we think of acting as dashing about all over the place, being busy: but true acting comes from falling quiet, watching the situation and then knowing what to do, if something shows itself as needing to be done.

'The law arises out of the fact.' Let us take an example from the last chapter: the case of the little boy who climbed through a hole in the fence on to an electric railway line. The fact was, said the Railway Board, that the little boy was a trespasser: he had no right to go on to their land. Out of that fact, they claimed, the law was they owed no duty to a trespasser who was injured by something dangerous on their property. Counsel for the little boy said, on the other hand, that the Railway Board had known for some time that their fences were broken down and also that children were accustomed to playing near the fence. On those facts, counsel said, the law was that the

British Railways Board did owe a duty of care to see that children did not wander on to the line. Which was right? How did the judges know?

No doubt they fell quiet and reflected on these two arguments. In doing so, reason would have presented the wholeness of the situation. It was true that the little boy was a trespasser; it was true also that perhaps parents should have been more careful to warn their children against the dangers of playing near the railway line. But when one looked at them as 'neighbours'—the little boy and the British Railways Board— the viewpoint changed. There was no comparison between their strengths and responsibilities. The Railway Board was a giant! And giants should be very careful where they tread, in case they crush small people!

Here we see how the viewpoint alters, from the level of reason. Reason comes from wholeness and unity. Watching from reason, when the mind is still, one sees the relationships between the parts making up the whole. Once the judges saw the relationship—that of being neighbours—there was no doubt what the law is. The law is, the strong owe a duty of care towards the weak.

Always the law works towards unity. We can see this in a criminal trial, where someone is charged with doing something wrong 'contrary to the peace of Our Sovereign Lady The Queen'. The prosecutor is said to be the Queen herself, because the peace of her people has been broken by what the man or woman has done. Now the effort is to restore that man or woman to the same peace: for, by his or her crime, the prisoner in the dock of the court has separated from the rest of the community. After a fair trial, to establish whether the crime was committed, it may be that the defendant will have to be punished. But if it has been a fair trial, and a jury of his peers has returned a verdict of 'Guilty', it often is the case that the defendant will accept his or her punishment and know that it is right; and, having been punished, will be restored to the general peace of his fellow-men.

No-one wants to be separate from others. That is why going to prison for committing a crime is so painful: for there one is not only deprived of the freedom to do one's proper work but also of the friendships which one normally enjoys. Through being locked away in a prison, it is hoped that he or she will learn a lesson and return to the community with a willingness to serve others, and be served, which is the unity of mankind.

So it is very important that a defendant in a criminal trial is not put away in prison unless a jury of twelve men and women, having heard all the evidence, return a verdict of 'Guilty'. The word 'verdict' means 'truly said'. A jury must not convict anyone of a crime unless they can truly say that he did it. They have to be sure of his guilt. The defendant is put in their charge, a jury of his peers, meaning 'equals'. When a man has pleaded 'Not Guilty' to a charge he is said to 'put himself upon his country': and the country is the jury, for they are his fellow-men. They only, not the judge, are the ones to decide whether he has committed an act which is bad enough to warrant shutting him off from the community.

The earliest juries were, in fact, neighbours of the defendant who could swear on oath about the facts of the case. Even today a jury is composed of men and women from the locality in which the crime took place. But they do not speak and give evidence: their task is to listen attentively to all the evidence that is presented to them, by Counsel for the Crown and for the Defence, and then decide whether the Crown has proved the defendant's guilt. It is not up to the defendant to prove that he is not guilty: if he wishes to he can remain silent throughout the trial. The burden of proof, as it is called, rests throughout the trial on the Crown.

Sir William Blackstone calls trial by jury 'the grand bulwark' of an Englishman's liberties. He says that these cannot be taken away from him except by the verdict of a jury: whereas, in other countries, a single judge or an official of government might decide to imprison a man or even send him to his death, simply because they did not like him. He warns that the same thing might happen here, unless we are careful:

So that the liberties of England cannot but subsist, so long as this palladium [the jury] remains sacred and inviolate, not only from open attacks . . . but also from all secret machinations, which may sap and undermine it; by introducing new and arbitrary methods of trial, by justices of the peace, commissioners of the revenue, and courts of conscience. And however *convenient* these may appear at first (as doubtless all arbitrary powers, well executed, are the most convenient) yet let it be again remembered, that delays, and little inconveniences in the forms of justice, are the price that all free nations must pay for their liberty in more substantial matters; that these inroads upon this sacred bulwark of the nation are fundamentally opposite to the spirit of our constitution; and that, though begun in trifles, the precedent may gradually increase and spread, to the utter disuse of juries in questions of the most momentous concern.

Fortunately, there is still every indication that juries value their independence and will not be told, even by a judge, what verdict they should bring in. Juries have had a sturdy history and have even been threatened by judges in the past with being locked up themselves if they did not return a verdict of 'Guilty'. Still they did not give in. When, centuries ago, men could be hung for stealing sheep, juries refused to convict prisoners in their charge—even when the case had been proved against them. Parliament had to take account of their views, and change the written law which was so harsh.

Today, serving on a jury is often the only time an ordinary man or woman takes part in the government of the nation. That is why the jury is such a valuable institution. Almost anyone over the age of eighteen is liable to be summoned to serve on a local jury for a short period: and when they do attend, most jurors find that it is a rewarding experience. For, whatever their own feelings and ideas and prejudices, they find that a jury takes on a life of its own, with its own body, mind and feelings, in which they participate. A verdict is the statement of the whole jury, not of its individual parts. They experience what it is like to be members of a greater body.

13
The Purpose of the State

> Without . . . civil society man could not by any possibility arrive
> at the perfection of which his nature is capable.–*Edmund Burke*

On our journey through the Constitution we have come a very
long way. But what does it all mean to us—to you and to me—
who live by this constitution? At the end of the line is the
ordinary person, for whom, it seems, all the mighty
institutions exist. There would be no use having a Monarch
and Parliament and Law Courts and a Church without the
people. The great officers of state serve us and we, in turn,
serve humanity by doing the work we are meant to do.

The purpose of the State is to provide the conditions in
which we can be truly happy: being truly happy means
performing those talents and skills which each of us has been
given, to the glory of God, and the enrichment of mankind.

There is a story about Jesus, with which you are probably
familiar. Men were always trying to trap him by his own words,
so that they could prove he was not the Son of God, as He
claimed. One day they asked Him whether it was lawful to
serve Caesar, the Roman Emperor who ruled over Israel at the
time. Jesus knew, of course, that they wanted to hear Him say
that He was their only true king, and they should serve Him,
and not Caesar. They would then have taken Him before the
Roman authorities who would have punished Him for
disobedience to the Emperor.

Jesus asked them to show Him a piece of the money they
used to pay taxes to the Roman Emperor. They showed Him a
coin with a head and writing on it.

> And he saith unto them, Whose is this image and superscription?
> They say unto him, Caesar's. Then saith he unto them,

> Render therefore unto Caesar the things which are Caesar's;
> and unto God the things that are God's.

They really could not quarrel with that answer, and went away, no doubt to work out other ways of trapping Him. But what did the answer mean?

First of all, the word 'render' means 'to give back'. Therefore giving back to Caesar in taxes the money which Caesar himself had issued, with his own head on it, was very simple and natural: Caesar had made the money available in the first place so that trade could take place, and men could be happy in the trust that Caesar would stand behind the coins he issued and honour them. They could be sure that the money was good; therefore they did not always have to worry. More trade and more business could take place, when the currency was stable. Men would be happier and more prosperous and, in those conditions, it was likely they would render, or give back, the talents which God had given them: glorifying and magnifying God through their works. Mankind would thus be enriched and lifted towards the Creator.

In a sense, Jesus turned the tables very neatly on his opponents. All that the State asked for, in the person of Caesar, the Emperor, was the return of some of the money that it had created, in return for which it would continue to give protection. But what was to be rendered to God was a man's whole life and service–an altogether greater and finer thing.

We are meant to glorify God through our works. This is the journey which the Self takes in the chariot of the body. In working for each other, unselfishly, men find that true happiness which is the nature of their Creator. Sir William Blackstone said:

> [the Creator] has not perplexed the law of nature with a
> multitude of abstract rules and precepts . . . but has graciously
> reduced the rule of obedience to this one paternal precept,
> 'that man should pursue his own happiness'.

And Jean Domat tells us, in beautiful and measured words:

Thus without Man, the heavens, the stars, the light, the air, are objects which present themselves to Mankind, as a good common to them all, and of which every person hath the entire use. And all the things which the earth and the waters bear or bring forth, are likewise of common use; but in such a manner, that not any one of them passes to our use, but by the labour of many persons. And this renders men necessary to one another, and forms among them the different ties for the uses of agriculture, commerce, arts, sciences, and for all the other communications which the several wants of life may depend.

In government, the sovereign, which is the Queen in Parliament, must always act so as to secure justice and peace, for these are what the people require if they are to fulfil themselves. Justice comes before peace; for sometimes it is necessary to go to war to secure justice. And justice does not mean treating everyone equally—but treating them as they need and deserve. There is a famous description of justice: it is 'the constant and everlasting will to render to every one his due'. It is commonly thought that justice means what a man gets if he does wrong and offends the State. But it is altogether much bigger than that: what is due to a man is what is necessary to perform his talents and skills. King Alfred was right when he said that men were his tools to do the work he was charged to perform: namely, to build a nation. And that they required, in their various orders, materials to sustain them and to work on, such as land, which the King should supply.

Peace is important, for in peace men can perform their true work. The true meaning of peace is that it binds men together, whereas war divides them. And peace has to be guarded, for it is a very precious possession. We speak of the 'Queen's Peace' when we refer to quietness and good order throughout the kingdom. A policeman is an officer of the peace, for he acts to prevent it being broken. There are justices of the peace sitting in towns whose work it is to maintain the peace of the area in which they live, and to award penalties against troublemakers.

For many centuries these justices, worthy men of the area, did all the work of government that was required: they directed the repair of roads and bridges, they looked after the poor and they kept the peace. So government was simple and direct. And even until quite recently it has been well said that, in England, the only people connected with government that ordinary men and women met were the policeman and the postman!

Honour is vital to the government of a state. Those who govern us must behave honourably, for they set an example to us all. Honour means respect or esteem; and we give respect and esteem to someone who deserves it by the excellence of his or her conduct. For example, we greatly respect the Queen, whose life and rule over us are both above reproach: she is always pleasant and courteous; she is attentive to everyone; she never complains about the work she has to do; and she never allows personal comfort or gain to swallow up her duty to the nation.

A few years ago the President of the United States of America, one of the most powerful heads of state in the world today, tried to protect himself and his friends from punishment for a silly crime they had got involved in. He was found out and had to give up his great office: for he had dishonoured himself and the people he led. If he had been allowed to continue as President, all Americans would have suffered, because none of them would have been able to trust his leadership. Fear and doubt as to what was right would have spread among the people.

And all other holders of office in the government of a state must be honourable men and women, and not work for their own benefit but for the good of the people. Privy Councillors who, as we have seen, are trusted men and women close to the Queen, are called 'Right Honourable' simply because their conduct of affairs is, or should be, of the highest order. Unfortunately, from time to time, a few of them abuse the trust which is placed in them.

The Australians had a Prime Minister a few years ago who thought he was above the law: he was becoming a tyrant. A tyrant is someone who thinks he alone knows what is best for the people in his charge, and can dictate laws to them. Australia is a country which follows our system of government. The Queen is Queen of Australia. But, because the Queen has to spend most of her time here, in the British Isles, she needs a 'viceroy' (which means 'in place of the King') to represent her. And so the practice has grown up of the Prime Minister of Australia recommending to the Queen a very eminent Australian to serve as Governor-General.

This Prime Minister, Mr Whitlam, asked the Queen in 1974 to appoint Sir John Kerr, a respected judge, as Governor-General. Soon after taking office, it became apparent to Sir John that there was growing resistance in the country to Mr Whitlam's high-handed ways of government: the people were becoming bitterly divided. Even if Mr Whitlam thought that his ideas would, in the end, benefit the country, he was trying to put them into effect at the cost of making a great many people angry.

Matters got so bad that, in 1975, the Senate, or upper house of the Australian Parliament, refused to grant Mr Whitlam the money he needed to carry on the affairs of government. Imagine, if you will, what it would be like here if there was no money to pay the policemen and the army and the judges and all the other servants of the state. In such a situation, where a Prime Minister cannot get the taxes to support his government, the honourable thing for him to do is to resign, together with his ministers, and ask the people in an election whether they are willing to 'render unto him', or someone else, the necessary money for affairs of state. But Mr Whitlam refused to resign.

The Governor-General, a great and a good man, was very troubled by the situation. He saw the deadlock between the Senate and the House of Representatives, which is what the Australians call their House of Commons, over the supply of money as a reflection of the deep division in the state. This is a terrible ordeal for any country, for it means that nothing can be done at all for the good of its people. You perhaps know what it is like when you are full of fear and doubt, and there is no-one to tell you what is the right thing to do: you feel powerless to act, helpless. So it is on a much larger scale, and with more dreadful consequences, when a whole state is left without proper government: the various parts which go to make up the whole may start to war with each other, and destroy each other and the wholeness of the nation to which they belong.

Fortunately, as we have learned, the Queen has 'prerogative power'. The word 'prerogative' means 'before, or beyond, question'. The power which is beyond question is that which is unlimited, that is, the power of God to do right. The Queen has this power only to do right for her people, and never to do wrong. In the situation facing Sir John Kerr, the Governor-General, and the Queen's representative in Australia, that power was needed to act to resolve the deadlock.

After consulting the Chief Justice of Australia, Sir John Kerr exercised the prerogative power. He called Mr Whitlam to his study on 11 November 1975. He first asked the Prime Minister whether he still intended to try and govern without money voted by the Australian Parliament. Whitlam said 'Yes'. The Governor-General then dismissed him as Prime Minister, and the other ministers in his cabinet.

Mr Whitlam jumped up and said he wanted to get in touch with the Queen at once. Having advised the Queen to appoint Sir John Kerr as Governor-General, Mr Whitlam thought he might be able to get Her Majesty to undo the appointment: but he was too late. Sir John had already signed the letter of dismissal.

Later, on the steps of Parliament House, the Governor-General's Secretary read a proclamation dissolving Parliament, ready for a new election. Mr Whitlam was present in the huge crowd. The Secretary ended the proclamation with the words 'God save the Queen!' Mr Whitlam said: 'Well may we say God save the Queen, because nothing will save the Governor-General.' This was a terrible thing to say because, even if he did not agree with what the Governor-General had done, he should not have tried to whip up fury in the crowd, which would only cause further pain and suffering. Yet this is what he tried to do: 'Maintain your rage,' he told his followers.

However, in no less than two elections which followed the Governor-General's action, Mr Whitlam was rejected as Prime Minister by the people. Then he was forced to retire as leader of his party, the Labour Party of Australia. So good sense prevailed: but not until much damage had been done. And it is ever necessary to be on the alert for, and challenge, men who try to govern us tyrannically.

How did the Governor-General know how to do right?

Again it was necessary to fall still and quiet. He had to watch and wait. He observed what was going on in government for well over a year. Then, when nothing was happening at all, and the people were helpless and troubled, he knew what he had to do: it was very simple and very direct, he dismissed the Prime Minister. That was all: or very nearly all, for there had to be another man ready and willing to take on the post of Prime Minister until an election could be called. Such a man was available, who agreed to serve responsibly.

Nor was it the act of a dictator or tyrant. Sir John Kerr simply acted to unlock the people's own ability to do what they knew to be right. He left it for them to decide, in an election, whether they wanted Mr Whitlam to continue as Prime Minister.

A letter was written soon afterwards to Her Majesty the Queen by a supporter of Mr Whitlam asking her to intervene and restore him to office. The Queen replied through her Private Secretary, 'Her Majesty, as Queen of Australia, is watching events in Canberra [the capital city of Australia] with close interest and attention, but it would not be proper for her to intervene in person in matters which are so clearly placed within the jurisdiction of the Governor-General. . .'

This letter is interesting. Notice how the Private Secretary describes the Queen as 'watching events . . . with close interest and attention'. This is the part the monarch plays: always alert and vigilant for the good of her people, and only intervening—at a very high level in the mind of the nation—when it is absolutely necessary. That kind of action will always be simple, clear and direct, but it will always have the greatest effect. In the analogy of the chariot, it is when the charioteer pulls the rein slightly and thus turns the horses and the chariot away from the road which leads to destruction.

Sir John Kerr behaved honourably, with no thought for his personal benefit. Indeed, had Mr Whitlam been re-elected as Prime Minister, nothing would have saved the Governor-General. Whitlam would have asked the Queen to appoint someone else. As it was, the supporters of Whitlam afterwards acted disgracefully towards the Queen's representative: they insulted him, they threw yellow paint over his car while he was travelling in it and they arranged riots wherever the Governor-General was going to be. Finally, in 1977, Sir John Kerr resigned—again in the interests of the Australian people, so that peace would surround the office of Governor-General.

So to do right, honourably and courageously, does not always mean that one is going to be popular. It may bring insult and humiliation. Yet it has to be done, for evil will triumph over men's minds if good men do nothing. Taking a stand, as Sir John Kerr did, halts the flow of evil and turns men's hearts and minds towards the good.

It may well happen, in times to come, that our own Queen or King will have to act to protect the Constitution. That is a very great and serious act to have to perform. When and if it does occur, there are three things to remember: first, that the monarch should not be prevented from acting; second, that he or she has a *duty* to act in such circumstances; and third, that he or she will need the support of right-thinking men and women.

Far better is it now for all of us to try to understand and love and work for the Constitution by which we live, so that such a crisis does not arise. The English love freedom. What is freedom? It comes, as we have seen, from two words: 'doom' meaning 'law or place'; and 'free', meaning 'dear' or 'friend'. Freedom means the law of friends, which requires serving and helping each other without thought of personal gain.

Epilogue

The book that you have just read is all about the riches and the glories of the English Constitution. In some respects it has been like looking at coloured slides projected on to a wall, with vivid scenes of coronations and uniforms and glittering jewels and judges in their red robes. Much of this you can see for yourselves, in London, today: and, indeed, you should take every opportunity to visit the places and scenes described, such as Westminster Abbey, the Changing of the Guard, the Houses of Parliament and the Royal Courts of Justice.

Plato in *The Republic* describes most of us as spending our lives chained to a kind of cinema seat watching reflections being played on a big screen in front of us. Someone is always responsible for operating the projector. And they are the images presented to us of the ideas and the beliefs of men of the past. Some of the images, such as those illustrated in this book, are rich, pleasant and worthwhile; others, coming from the minds of men with evil intent, are horrifying and lead to nightmares. But they are all, good and bad, just reflections.

Much more rewarding is to approach the reality behind all the changing scenes. Plato describes this, too, when he speaks of a man in the audience escaping from his chains and going out into the sunlight of reason. That, of course, means work and study: and it really is the study and the growing appreciation of the unchanging laws which lie behind the reflections.

So, if you have enjoyed this introductory book, make up your mind to pursue the study of citizenship. No doubt you will have a diet of books to read in the next few years, to pass examinations and perhaps go to university. But, to assist you to penetrate this great constitution of ours there is set out, in a following Appendix, a list of books which you will find most useful. Do try to read them.

Old Judge Coke in the seventeenth century had some good advice for a student:

> . . . that first he read again and again (a section of a book) and do his best endeavours, first of himself, and then by conference with others (which is the life of study) to understand it . . . and no more at any one time than he is able with a delight to bear away, and after to meditate thereon, which is the life of reading . . . . And albeit the reader shall not at any one day (do what he can) reach to the meaning of the author . . . yet let him in no way discourage himself, but proceed; for on some other day, in some other place, that doubt will be cleared.

Appendix 1

We have read in this book some of the words of great statesmen, judges and writers which have helped to shape the English Constitution. Here are some more readings, collected together roughly in order of time, to help us appreciate the riches of language which have gone into the formation of the English character and government.

1. A letter from King Alfred to his bishops

Alfred, who ruled from 871 to 901, found time in the cares of state to devote himself to the translation of works into English, so that education might uplift the new nation:

> . . . I also remembered how, before everything was ravaged and burnt, the churches throughout all England stood filled with treasures and books, and likewise there was a great multitude of the servants of God. And they had very little benefit from those books, for they could not understand anything in them, because they were not written in their own language. As if they had said: 'Our forefathers who formerly held these monasteries loved wisdom, and through it they obtained wealth and left it to us. Their track can still be seen, but we cannot follow it up, and we have now lost both the wealth and the wisdom, because we were unwilling to incline our mind to that track.'
>
> When I remembered all this, I wondered exceedingly at those good and wise men who were in former times throughout England, and had fully studied all those books, that they would not turn any part of them into their own language. But then at once I answered myself and said: 'They did not think that men would ever become so careless and learning so decayed; they abstained intentionally, wishing that here in the land there should be the greater wisdom, the more languages we knew.'
>
> Then I remembered also how the divine law was first

composed in the Hebrew language, and afterwards, when the Greeks learnt it, they turned it all into their own language, and also all other books. And the Romans likewise, when they had learnt them, turned them all through learned interpreters into their own language. And also all other Christian nations turned some part of them into their own language. Therefore it seems better to me, if it seems so to you, that we also should turn into the language that we can all understand some books, which may be most necessary for all men to know; and bring to pass, as we can very easily with God's help, if we have the peace, that all the youth now in England, born of free men who have the means that they can apply to it, may be devoted to learning as long as they cannot be of use in any other employment, until such time as they can read well what is written in English.

2. John of Salisbury on the difference between a prince and a tyrant

John, a learned man, and a lover of Plato, lived in the twelfth century in the reign of that great king, Henry II. John wrote, in 1159, a famous book on government, entitled *Policraticus*:

> Between a tyrant and a prince there is this single or chief difference, that the latter obeys the law and rules the people by its dictates, accounting himself as but their servant. It is by virtue of the law that he makes good his claim to the foremost and chief place in the management of the affairs of the commonwealth and in the bearing of its burdens; and his elevation over others consists in this, that whereas private men are held responsible only for their private affairs, on the prince fall the burdens of the whole community. Wherefore deservedly there is conferred on him, and gathered together in his hands, the power of all his subjects, to the end that he may be sufficient unto himself in seeking and bringing about the advantage of each individually, and of all; and to the end that the state of the human commonwealth may be ordered in the best possible manner, seeing that each and all are members one of another. Wherein we indeed but follow nature, the best guide of life; for nature has gathered together all the senses of her microcosm or little world, which is man, into the head, and has subjected all the members in obedience to it in such wise

that they will all function properly so long as they follow the guidance of the head. . .

3. Magna Carta
Most Englishmen have heard of Magna Carta, or the Great Charter of Liberties, even if they do not know what is in it. They believe that it gave them certain rights. The Charter was signed by King John, under pressure from the barons, in 1215. The following two 'chapters' are certainly of great importance:

> 39. No free man shall be taken or imprisoned or dispossessed, or outlawed, or banished, or in any way destroyed, nor will we go upon him, nor send upon him, except by the legal judgment of his peers or by the law of the land.
> 40. To no one will we sell, to no one will we deny, or delay, right or justice.

4. Bracton on a king's wisdom
The lawyer and judge, Bracton, wrote *On the Laws and Customs of England* in the middle of the thirteenth century. Here is another reading from that work:

> Nothing is more fitting for a sovereign than to live by the laws, nor is there any greater sovereignty than to govern according to law, and he ought properly to yield to the law what the law has bestowed on him, for the law makes him king. And since it is not only necessary that the king be armed with weapons and laws but with wisdom, let the king learn wisdom that he may maintain justice, and God will grant wisdom to him, and when he has found it he will be blessed if he holds to it, for there is honour and glory in the speech of the wise and the tongue of the imprudent is its own overthrow; the government of the wise man is stable, and the wise king will judge his people, but if he lacks wisdom he will destroy them, for from a corrupt head corruption descends to the members, and if understanding and virtue do not flourish in the head it follows that the other members cannot perform their functions.

5. Writ of summons for a Parliament
Here is an example of an early writ of summons, issued by

Edward I, calling together first the clergy, led by the Archbishop of Canterbury, then the barons, followed by representatives of the counties and boroughs, in 1295. Only a brief extract is given:

> The king to the venerable father in Christ Robert, by the same grace archbishop of Canterbury, primate of all England, greeting. As a most just law, established by the careful providence of sacred princes, exhorts and decrees that what affects all, by all should be approved, so also, very evidently should common danger be met by means provided in common. . .

> The king to the sheriff of Northamptonshire (and likewise to all other counties). Since we intend to have a consultation and meeting with the earls, barons and other principal men of our kingdom with regard to providing remedies against the dangers which are in these days threatening the same kingdom; and on that account have commanded them to be with us on the Lord's day next after the feast of St Martin in the approaching winter, at Westminster, to consider, ordain, and do as may be necessary for the avoidance of these dangers; we strictly require you to cause two knights from the aforesaid county, two citizens from each city in the same county, and two burgesses from each borough, of those who are especially discreet and capable of labouring, to be elected without delay, and cause them to come to us at the aforesaid time and place.

6. Fortescue on the king's rule
Chief Justice Fortescue, exiled in the civil war which tormented the country in the mid-fifteenth century, wrote a dialogue between himself and the young Prince Edward, son of Henry VI, called *In Praise of the Laws of England*. It was intended to restore sanity to the warring nobles and remind them of their traditions:

> . . . The king of England is not able to change the laws of his kingdom at pleasure, for he rules his people with a government not only regal but also political. If he were to preside over them with a power entirely regal, he would be able to change the laws of his realm, and also to impose on them tallages and other

burdens without consulting them. This is the sort of dominion which the Civil Laws indicate when they state 'What has pleased the prince has the force of law'. But the case is far otherwise with the king who rules his people politically, because he is not able himself to change the laws without the assent of his subjects, nor to burden an unwilling people with strange imposts. Thus, ruled by laws which they themselves desire, they freely enjoy their properties and are despoiled neither by their own king nor by any other.

Indeed, the people rejoice in the same way under a king who rules entirely regally, provided that he does not degenerate into a tyrant. Of such a king Aristotle said in his *Politics*, that 'It is better for a city to be ruled by the best man than by the best law'. But, because it does not always happen that the man who presides over a people is of this sort, St Thomas, in the book he wrote for the king of Cyprus, is considered to have desired that a kingdom be constituted in such a way that the king may not be free to govern his people tyrannically which only comes to pass when the regal power is restrained by political law.

7. The case of prohibitions

But, in the seventeenth century, the Stuart kings, first James and then Charles, foolishly began to try to override Parliament. They became arrogant and tyrannical. When James I said that he was every bit as capable as his own judges to try causes, even when they were concerned with disputes between himself and his subjects, Chief Justice Coke very courageously and firmly told him he was wrong (1607):

> . . . then the king said, that he thought the law was founded on reason, and that he and others had reason, as well as the judges: to which it was answered by me, that true it was, that God had endowed his Majesty with excellent science, and great endowments of nature; but his Majesty was not learned in the laws of his realm of England, and causes which concern the life, or inheritance, or goods, or fortunes of his subjects, are not to be decided by natural reason but by the artificial reason and judgment of law, which law is an act which requires long study and experience, before that a man can attain to the cognizance of it: and that the law was the golden met-wand and measure to

try the causes of the subjects; and which protected his Majesty
in safety and peace: with which the king was greatly offended,
and said, that then he should be under the law, which was
treason to affirm, as he said; to whom I said, that Bracton saith,
'the king must be under no man, but under God and the law'.

8. The Petition of Right

Charles I tried to tax his subjects without the consent of
Parliament; he imprisoned people without giving reasons; he
imposed law through his soldiers. All of which caused
Parliament to draw up a Petition of Right (1628), protesting
against the King's excesses:

> They do therefore humbly pray your Most Excellent Majesty,
> that no man hereafter be compelled to make or yield any gift,
> loan, benevolence, tax, or such like charge, without common
> consent by Act of Parliament; and that none be called to make
> answer, or take such oath, or to give attendance, or be
> confined, or otherwise molested or disquieted concerning the
> same, or for refusal thereof; and that no freeman, in any such
> manner as is before-mentioned, be imprisoned or detained;
> and that Your Majesty will be pleased to remove the said
> soldiers and mariners, and that your people may not be so
> burdened in time to come; and that the aforesaid commissions
> for proceeding by martial law, may be revoked and annulled;
> and that hereafter no commissions of like nature may issue
> forth to any person or persons whatsoever, to be executed as
> aforesaid, lest by colour of them any of your Majesty's subjects
> be destroyed or put to death, contrary to the laws and franchise
> of the land.
>
> All which they most humbly pray of your Most Excellent
> Majesty, as their rights and liberties according to the laws and
> statutes of this realm; and that your Majesty would also
> vouchsafe to declare, that the awards, doings, and proceedings
> to the prejudice of your people, in any of the premises, shall
> not be drawn hereafter into consequence or example: and that
> your Majesty would also be graciously pleased, for the further
> comfort and safety of your people, to declare your royal will
> and pleasure, that in the things aforesaid all your officers and
> ministers shall serve you, according to the laws and statutes of

this realm, as they tender the honour of your Majesty, and the prosperity of this kingdom.

The King sent a reply agreeing to the requests:

> The King willeth that right be done according to the laws and customs of the realm; and that the statutes be put in due execution, that his subjects may have no cause to complain of any wrong or oppressions, contrary to their just rights and liberties, to the preservation whereof he holds himself as well obliged as of his prerogative.

9. The trial of King Charles

Charles would not learn his lesson and a civil war was fought to make the point that the King was not above the law. In 1649 the King was put on trial for high treason by the House of Commons, and later was sentenced to death. He put up a spirited defence:

> *The King*: England was never an elective kingdom but an hereditary kingdom for near these thousand years; therefore let me know by what authority I am called hither. I do stand more for the liberty of my people than any here that come to be my lawful judges.
> *Lord President*: Sir, how really you have managed your trust is known. Your way of answer is to interrogate the Court, which beseems not you in your condition.
> *The King*: I do not come here as submitting to the Court. Yet I will stand as much for the privilege of the House of Commons, rightly understood, as any man here whatsoever. But I see no House of Lords here that may constitute a Parliament. Is this the bringing of the King to his Parliament? Is this the bringing to an end of the treaty in the public faith of the world? Let me see a legal authority warranted by the Word of God, the Scriptures, or warranted by the constitutions of the kingdom, and I will answer.

10. A written constitution

Oliver Cromwell, 'Lord Protector' after the death of Charles, gave us our only written constitution, *The Instrument of Government*, in 1653. It lasted only about six years:

The government of the Commonwealth of England, Scotland, and Ireland, and the dominions thereunto belonging:

I. That the supreme legislative authority of the Commonwealth of England, Scotland, and Ireland, and the dominions thereunto belonging, shall be and reside in one person, and the people assembled in Parliament; the style of which person shall be the Lord Protector of the Commonwealth of England, Scotland, and Ireland.

II. That the exercise of the chief magistracy and the administration of the government over the said countries and the dominions, and the people thereof, shall be in the Lord Protector, assisted with a council, the number whereof shall not exceed twenty-one, nor be less than thirteen. . .

11. The Bill of Rights

The Stuarts, having been restored to the throne in 1660, were soon at their old tricks; and when the unpopular James II fled the country in 1688 Parliament drew up a Bill of Rights to prevent further abuses of power by a monarch. The Stuarts had been particularly fond of 'suspending' laws, or 'dispensing' with them, whenever it suited their own purposes: thus putting themselves above the law, contrary to what Bracton had stated:

> . . . And thereupon the said lords spiritual and temporal and commons pursuant to their respective letters and elections being now assembled in a full and free representative of this nation, taking into their most serious consideration the best means for attaining the ends aforesaid, do in the first place (as their ancestors in like case have usually done) for the vindicating and asserting their ancient rights and liberties, declare:
>
> That the pretended power of suspending of laws or the execution of laws by regal authority without consent of parliament is illegal.
>
> That the pretended power of dispensing with laws or the execution of laws by regal authority as it hath been assumed and exercised of late is illegal.
>
> That the commission for erecting the late court of commissioners for ecclesiastical causes and all other commissions and courts of like nature are illegal and pernicious.

That the levying money for or to the use of the crown by pretence of prerogative without grant of parliament for a longer time or in other manner than the same is or shall be granted is illegal.

That it is the right of subjects to petition the king and all commitments and prosecutions for such petitioning are illegal.

That the raising or keeping a standing army within the kingdom in time of peace unless it be with consent of parliament is against law.

That the subjects which are Protestants may have arms for their defence suitable to their conditions and as allowed by law.

That election of members of parliament ought to be free.

That the freedom of speech and debates or proceedings in parliament ought not to be impeached or questioned in any court or place out of parliament.

That excessive bail ought not to be required nor excessive fines imposed nor cruel and unusual punishments inflicted. . .

And that for redress of all grievances and for the amending, strengthening and preserving of the laws parliaments ought to be held frequently.

And they do claim, demand and insist upon all and singular the premises as their undoubted rights and liberties and that no declarations, judgments, doings or proceedings to the prejudice of the people in any of the said premises ought in any wise to be drawn hereafter into consequence or example. . .

12. Blackstone and the Common Law
'Twice in the history of English law has an Englishman had the motive, the courage, the power, to write a great, readable, reasonable book about English law as a whole. First it was Bracton, and five hundred years later Blackstone.' He collected together the law, made it known and showed the reason for it:

That ancient collection of unwritten maxims and customs, which is called the common law, however compounded, or from whatever fountains derived, had subsisted immemorially in this kingdom; and, though somewhat altered and impaired by the violence of the times, had in great measure weathered the rude shock of the Norman conquest. This had endeared it to the people in general, as well because its decisions were universally known, as because it was found to be excellently adapted to the genius of the English nation. . .

13. Burke and the Constitution

Edmund Burke (1729–97) was a great voice of reason in the eighteenth century. His book *Reflections on the Revolution in France*, read widely here and in Europe, gave strength and wisdom to resist violent attacks on the constitution, which came at the end of the century. Burke thought the constitution could be modified, if one knew what one was doing, but not undermined. In the following extract he speaks of the English having, in their constitution, 'an invaluable treasure':

> They are not, I think, without some causes of apprehension and complaint; but these they do not owe to their Constitution, but to their own conduct. I think our happy situation owing to our Constitution—but owing to the whole of it, and not to any part singly—owing in a great measure to what we have left standing in our several reviews and reformations, as well as to what we have altered or superadded. Our people will find employment enough for a truly patriotic, free, and independent spirit, in guarding what they possess from violation. I would not exclude alteration neither; but even when I changed, it should be to preserve. I should be led to my remedy by a great grievance. In what I did, I should follow the example of our ancestors. I would make the reparation as nearly as possible in the style of the building . . . [Our forefathers] acted under a strong impression of the ignorance and fallibility of mankind. He that had made them thus fallible rewarded them for having in their conduct attended to their nature. Let us imitate their caution, if we wish to deserve their fortune or retain their bequests. Let us add, if we please, but let us preserve what they have left. . .

14. The Reform Act, 1832

This was the first of a series of Acts to extend the vote in elections for Members of Parliament: it gave the vote to small landowners, tenants and shopkeepers. Now, of course, almost everyone over the age of 18 has the right to vote. Lord Macaulay spoke in the House of Commons in March 1831:

Turn where we may, within, around, the voice of great events is proclaiming to us, Reform, that you may preserve. Now, therefore, while everything at home and abroad forbodes ruin to those who persist in a hopeless struggle against the spirit of the age; now, while the crash of the proudest throne of the continent is still resounding in our ears; now, while the roof of a British palace affords an ignominious shelter to the exiled heir of forty kings; now, while we see on every side ancient institutions subverted and great societies dissolved; now, while the heart of England is still sound; now, while old feelings and old associations retain a power and a charm which may soon pass away; now, in this your accepted time; now, in this your day of salvation, take counsel, not of prejudice, not of party spirit, not of the ignominious pride of a fatal consistency, but of history, of reason, of the ages which are past, of the signs of this most portentous time. . . If this bill be rejected, I pray to God that none of those who concur in rejecting it may ever remember their votes with unavailing remorse amidst the wreck of laws, the confusion of ranks, the spoliation of property, and the dissolution of social order.

15. Bagehot on the Monarchy
One of the most readable, intelligent and influential books on the English Constitution is that of the nineteenth-century author and journalist, Walter Bagehot:

The best reason why Monarchy is a strong government is, that it is an intelligible government. The mass of mankind understand it, and they hardly anywhere in the world understand any other. It is often said that men are ruled by their imaginations; but it would be truer to say that they are governed by the weakness of their imaginations. The nature of a constitution, the action of an assembly, the play of parties, the unseen formation of a guiding opinion, are complex facts, difficult to know and easy to mistake. But the action of a single will, the fiat of a single mind, are easy ideas: anybody can make them out, and no one can ever forget them. When you put before the mass of mankind the question 'Will you be governed by a king, or will you be governed by a constitution?' the inquiry comes out thus—'Will you be governed in a way you understand, or will you be governed in a way you do not understand?'

16. Dicey on the Rule of Law

Probably the greatest statement of the legal principles of the English Constitution came from Professor Dicey, also writing in the late nineteenth-century. We turn to his book *The Law of the Constitution* for the definition of the Rule of Law:

> When we say that the supremacy or the rule of law is a characteristic of the English constitution, we generally include under one expression at least three distinct though kindred conceptions.
>
> We mean, in the first place, that no man is punishable or can be lawfully made to suffer in body or goods except for a distinct breach of law established in the ordinary legal manner before the ordinary Courts of the land. In this sense the rule of law is contrasted with every system of government based on the exercise by persons in authority of wide, arbitrary, or discretionary powers of constraint. . .
>
> We mean in the second place . . . not only that with us no man is above the law, but (what is a different thing) that here every man, whatever be his rank or condition, is subject to the ordinary law of the realm and amenable to the jurisdiction of the ordinary tribunals. . .
>
> There remains yet a third and a different sense in which the 'rule of law' or the predominance of the legal spirit may be described as a special attribute of English institutions. We may say that the constitution is pervaded by the rule of law on the ground that the general principles of the constitution (as for example the right to personal liberty, or the right of public meeting) are with us the result of judicial decisions determining the rights of private persons in particular cases brought before the Courts; whereas under many foreign constitutions the security (such as it is) given to the rights of individuals results, or appears to result, from the general principles of the constitution.

17. The Parliament Act, 1911

The great clash between the House of Lords and the Commons came in 1909 with the rejection by the Lords of the

'People's Budget'. It was felt that the power of the Lords had to be curbed—especially with regard to money matters. Note that the preamble of the Act speaks of replacing the House of Lords: still not done, seventy years later!

Whereas it is expedient that provision should be made for regulating the relations between the two Houses of Parliament:

And whereas it is intended to substitute for the House of Lords as it at present exists a Second Chamber constituted on a popular instead of hereditary basis, but such substitution cannot be immediately brought into operation:

Be it therefore enacted by the King's most Excellent Majesty, by and with the advice and consent of the Lords Spiritual and Temporal, and Commons, in this present Parliament assembled, and by the authority of the same, as follows:

1(1) If a Money Bill, having been passed by the House of Commons, and sent up to the House of Lords at least one month before the end of the session, is not passed by the House of Lords without amendment within one month after it is so sent up to that House, the Bill shall, unless the House of Commons direct to the contrary, be presented to His Majesty and become an Act of Parliament on the Royal Assent being signified, notwithstanding that the House of Lords have not consented to the Bill. . .

2(1) If any Public Bill (other than a Money Bill or a Bill containing any provision to extend the maximum duration of Parliament beyond five years) is passed by the House of Commons in three successive sessions (whether of the same Parliament or not), and, having been sent up to the House of Lords at least one month before the end of the session, is rejected by the House of Lords in each of those sessions, that Bill shall, on its rejection for the third time by the House of Lords, unless the House of Commons direct to the contrary, be presented to His Majesty and become an Act of Parliament on the Royal Assent being signified thereto, notwithstanding that the House of Lords have not consented to the Bill: Provided that this provision shall not take effect unless two years have elapsed between the date of the second reading in the first of those sessions of the Bill in the House of Commons and the date on which it passes the House of Commons in the third of those sessions. . .

(*Note*: The Parliament Act, 1949, made it one year instead of two years.)

18. Lord Denning and Freedom under the Law

Lord Denning has done more than anyone else this century to bring home to us the essential qualities of our constitution. His book *Freedom under the Law* contains this classic statement about the duties of an individual:

> The freedom of the individual, which is so dear to us, has to be balanced with his duty; for, to be sure every one owes a duty to the society of which he forms part. The balance has changed remarkably during the last 100 years. Previously the freedom of the individual carried with it a freedom to acquire and use his property as he wished, a freedom to contract and so forth: but these freedoms were so much abused that in our time they have been counterbalanced by the duty to use one's property and powers for the good of society as a whole. In some foreign countries this duty has been carried to such a pitch that freedom, as we know it, no longer exists. If the people of those countries choose to put up with such a system that is their affair. All that needs to be said about it is that it is not the English view of human society. What matters in England is that each man should be free to develop his own personality to the full: and the only duties which should restrict this freedom are those which are necessary to enable everyone else to do the same. . .

Appendix 2

Further Reading

Bagehot, Walter, *The English Constitution* (Fontana paperback)

Blackstone, Sir William, *Commentaries on the Laws of England*, Vol. 1 (especially the Introduction); Vol. II, Chap. I; Vol. IV, Chap. 33

Burke, Edmund, *Reflections on the Revolution in France* (Everyman)

Chrimes, S.B., *English Constitutional History* (Oxford paperback)

de Smith, S.A., *Constitutional and Administrative Law* (Penguin)

Denning, Lord, *Freedom under the Law* (Stevens/Hamlyn Trust)

Dicey, A.V., *The Law of the Constitution* and *Law and Public Opinion in England* (Macmillan)

Strathearn Gordon, *Our Parliament* (Cassell)

Nicolson, Harold, *King George V* (Constable)

Wheeler-Bennett, John, *King George VI* (Macmillan)

Some of these books will now only be available through the public libraries

References

Page   **Chapter 1**
1   The quotation which begins the chapter comes from
              Burke's 'Speech on Reform of Representation of the
              Commons in Parliament' (1782).
4   Blackstone, *Commentaries on the Laws of England*,
              Introduction, section 2.
5–6   *Crito*, 51 (Jowett translation).
7–8   *The Republic*, Bk II, 368–9.

              Chapter 2
9   Maria, Lady Callcott, *Little Arthur's History of England*,
              Century edn. (1975), p.30.
10ff.   The text drawn on is the Penguin Classic, *The Agricola
              and The Germania* (1970).
13   Bracton, *On the Laws and Customs of England*, trans.
              Thorne, ed. Woodbine (Harvard, 1968), Vol II, p.33.
14   Coke, *Prohibitions del Roy* (1607), 12 Co.Rep. 63.
14   Lord Denning, *Gouriet* v. *Union of Post Office Workers*
              (1977), 1 A.E.R. 718.
14–15   Quoted in *Life of Alfred the Great*, by Thomas Hughes
              (Macmillan, 1902), p.298.
15–16   From Alfred's version of Boethius: *English Historical
              Documents*, Vol. I (Eyre and Spottiswoode), pp.845–6.
17   *History of the English-Speaking Peoples* (Cassell), Vol. I,
              p.96.

              Chapter 3
18   *The Ten Principal Upanishads* (Faber, 1952), p.32.
19   Matthew 8:.5–9
25   Quoted in *Our Parliament*, by Strathearn Gordon
              (Cassell, for the Hansard Society, 1964), p.74.

28   *King George VI*, John Wheeler-Bennett (Macmillan, 1958), pp. 406–7.

Chapter 4
29   *Liber Regalis*: from *The English Coronation Service*, E.C. Ratcliffe (Skeffington, 1937), p.56.
30   Matthew 20: 26–8.
30   *Majesty*, Robert Lacey (Sphere edn.), p.198.
34   Burke, *Reflections on the Revolution in France*.
36   The summary is given on p.70 of *The English Coronation Service*, op.cit. Other books on the coronation include *The Coronation Service*, F.C.Eeeles (Mowbray, 1952) and *The Crown Jewels and Coronation Ritual* (Pitkin).
36–7 *King George VI*, op.cit., pp. 312–13.

Chapter 5
38   Sir William Blackstone, *Analysis of the Laws of England*, Chap. VI, 1.
39   *King George VI*, op.cit., pp. 565–6.
39   *Commentaries*, Bk I, Chap. 7.
39–40 *The English Constitution*, Walter Bagehot (Kegan Paul, 1882), introduction, p. xxxviii.
40–1 Bagehot, op.cit., pp. 75–6.
44   *Commentaries*, Bk I, Chap.5.

Chapter 6
47   Edmund Burke, 'Speech to Electors of Bristol' (1774).
49   *Ten Principal Upanishads*, op.cit., p.123.
50   The Speaker's words are quoted in Strathearn Gordon's *Our Parliament*, op.cit., p.ix. I am indebted to this excellent little book for its information. See also, *Parliament and Freedom*, Horace Maybray King (John Murray, 1966).

Chapter 7
57   Edmund Burke *Thoughts on the Cause of the Present Discontents* (1770).
61   *Heydon's Case* (1584), 3 Co. Rep. 7a.

62   *The Sayings of Lao-Tzu*, trans. Lionel Giles (John Murray), p.43.

62   Erskine May, *Parliamentary Practice*, 18th edn., p.676.

Chapter 8

69   *The English Constitution*, op. cit., p.90.

70   *Thoughts on Scarcity* (1795).

71   Description of the Opening of Parliament from *An Encyclopedia of Parliament* (Cassell, 1958).

71   'Speech on the Acts of Uniformity' (1772).

75   *Encyclopedia of Parliament*, op.cit., p.278.

77   'Appeal from the New to the Old Whigs' (1791).

Chapter 9

80   *Reflections on the Revolution in France.*

80–1   *On the Laws and Customs of England,* op.cit., Vol. II, p.33.

81   *Ten Principal Upanishads*, op.cit., pp.122–3.

82   Plato, *Laws*, Bk IV, 715.

83   *Christianity and Social Order* (Penguin, 1942), p.7.

83–4   *Commentaries*, Introduction, section 2.

84   Matthew 22: 35–40.

85   *The Civil Law in its Natural Order*, Vol. I, Chap. 1, section viii.

86   *Laws*, Bk I, 645.

86   The Common Law principle as to driving on the highway may be found expressed, e.g. per Atkin, L.J. in *Hambrook* v. *Stokes* (1925), 1 K.B. 141 at 156.

87   'Speech on Conciliation with America' (1775).

87   The judge was Hale, C.J. in *R.* v. *Taylor* (1676), 1 Vent. 293.

87   per Lord Sumner in *Bowman* v. *Secular Society* (1917), A.C. 406

88   Lord Atkin in *Donoghue* v. *Stevenson* (1932), A.C.562.

Chapter 10

90   Virgil, *Georgics*, ii, 698.

91   *Laws*, 864.

92   *The Road to Justice* (Stevens, 1955), p.4.
94–5   *History of the English People*, Chap. VI, section IV, 'The New Learning'.
97   *Civil Law in its Natural Order*, Introduction, Chap. IX.
98   Andrew MacLaren, House of Commons, February 1937.

Chapter 11
99   Preface to *Irish Reports*, (1674), quoted in *The Ancient Constitution and the Feudal Law*, J.G.A. Pocock (Cedric Chivers, 1974), p.41.
99   I Samuel 8.
100   *Commentaries*, Bk IV, Chap. 33.
101   Ulpian, Dig. 1.4.1.
102   *Commentaries*, Bk I, Introduction, section 3.
103   *Laws*, 645.
103–4   *Irish Reports*, op.cit., p.33 (Pocock).
104   *Laws*, 645.
105   Co. Litt., 97b.
106–7   *British Railways Board* v. *Herrington* (1972), 1 A.E.R. 749, H.L.
109   *Somersett's Case*, xx State Trials, 1.

Chapter 12
115–16 *Commentaries*, Bk IV, Chap. 27.

Chapter 13
117   Burke, *Reflections*
117–18 Matthew 22: 15–22.
118   *Commentaries*, Introduction, section 2.
119   Domat, *The Civil Law* . . . op.cit., Chap. II.
119   Justinian, *Institutions*, 1 i 1,
122   The events in the Governor-General's study are described on pp.358–9 of Sir John Kerr's book *Matters for Judgment* (Macmillan, 1979).
123   Sir John Kerr, op.cit., pp.374–5.

Appendix 1
Reading

1 *English Historical Documents*, Vol. 1, pp.818–19.
2 *The Statesman's Book* (Russell & Russell, NY, 1963), p.3.
3 *Select Documents of English Constitutional History*, ed. Adams and Stephens (Macmillan, NY, 1929), p.47.
4 *On the Laws and Customs of England*, op.cit., Vol. II, p.306.
5 *Select Documents*, op.cit., p.82.
6 *De Laudibus*, ed. S.B.Chrimes (Cambridge, 1942), pp.24–7.
7 12 Co. Rep. 63.
8 *Select Documents*, op.cit., pp.341–2.
9 *The Hollow Crown*, (French and Harrap, 1962), pp.43–4.
10 *Select Documents*, op.cit. p.407.
11 *Select Documents*, op.cit., pp.464–5.
12 *Commentaries*, Vol.I, Introduction, section 1.
13 *Reflections on the Revolution in France.*
14 *British Orations* (Everyman's Library, No.714), p.232.
15 *The English Constitution*, Chap. II.
16 *Introduction to the Study of the Law of the Constitution* (Macmillan, 1902), pp.183–4, 189, 191.
17 *Select Statutes, Cases and Documents* (Methuen, 1949), pp.351–2.
18 *Freedom under the Law* (Stevens/Hamlyn, 1949), pp.4–5.

Index